Skydiving

Skydiving

Thomas Fensch

New Century Books

Skydiving

Copyright © 2025 Thomas Fensch. All rights reserved. No part of this book may be reproduced or utilized in any form, or by any means, electronic or mechanical, including photocopying, recording or by any information storage or retrieval system without written permission of the publisher

New Century Books
Publishing trade books and e-books since January, 2000.
8821 Rockdale Rd.
N. Chesterfield, Va 23236

newcentbks@gmail.com

ISBN: 979-8-9888347-6-2 trade paperback

(reprint edition)

Front cover photo: Above Whidbey Island, Washington. No further identification or date shown.
Back cover photo: Navy free-fall team. No location or date shown.
Both photos courtesy of Pixabay.

"A MAD Look at Sky-diving" copyright ©1967 by E. C. Publications, Inc., is reprinted here by permission of MAD Magazine.

"Stimulus Addiction: The Sweet Psychic Jolt of Danger" by Bruce C. Ogilvie reprinted from Psychology Today Magazine. Used by permission of Doubleday & Co., Inc.

for George and Harriet McCulloch
and for Steve Rossetti

Contents

Preface ix

Acknowledgments. xiii

Introduction xv
    Why Jump Out of a Perfectly Good Airplane?
      By Steve Rossetti

The First Jump Experience 1

Stimulus Addiction: The Sweet Psychic Jolt of Danger. . . .13
    By Bruce C. Oglivie

The History of Sport Parachuting and Skydiving. 19

The Language of Parachuting and Skydiving 27

Questions and Answers 54

Personal Achievements 65

Poetry and Fiction
    Falling by James Dickey 76

    First Flight by Steven Osterlund 82

    Divers by Charles Ghigna. 82

    The Skydiver by jeannie McCombs 83

    The Phantom Tenth Man by Jim Rogers 84

    Skydiver by George McCulloch 87

    The Eternal Skydiver by Lori Spring............89
    The Man Who Flew Like a Bat by Martin Caidin.....93
    Peak Experience at 6:45 A.M. by Michael Horan...107
    A MAD Look at Sky Diving 113

Leaders in the Sport
    Captain Hook and the Sky Pirates...............126
    The Golden Knights 135
    Col. Joe Kittinger's Story 146
    Jerry Rouillard's Story 166
    jeanni McCombs and the Star Dusters............175
    George and Harriet McCulloch's Story 182

Epilogue: Make A Skydive 193
    by Dean Frazier

Appendix
    Sources 199

About the Author................................209

Preface

It is an *addicting* sport. Addicting in the best sense of that word. Addicting certainly, but a sport which, at times, seems out of synch with the beat of the rest of the sports world.

Like bullfighting, perhaps, skydiving has never really been accepted by the American public. Every skydiving fatality is covered on the front pages of the daily newspapers and every fatality is covered with the same cliches. Since the days of the barnstormers, skydiving has been an "outlaw sport"; pilots used to bail out to *survive*, those who did otherwise—who jumped for sport—soon heard all the standard lines . . . *only two things fall from the sky, birdshit and fools . . . whuffo you jump outta them planes for . . . my Mother didn't raise no fool . . .*

It has made some participants closet jumpers, reluctant to tell their family or friends that every Saturday and Sunday mornings, they jump from "perfectly good airplanes" for sport.

But it remains addicting, a siren call to those who appreciate it—a call for those who understand the air and how to fly in it—for those who love the feel, the rush, the camaraderie, the challenge, and the achievement of sport skydiving.

This book is for those who understand the sport, who jump first, and pay the rent later; for the Sunday jumper to the national competitor.

It is also for the families and friends of jumpers everywhere and for the countless *whuffo's* who know nothing of this modern space-age sport of the future.

This book is divided into three major parts: the first section explains the sport as a participant would enter the world of skydiving: through an introduction, then the first jump experience, then the addiction and hunger for more. Then we examine the language of jumping, the history, and the countless questions asked on every drop zone. Bruce C. Ogilvie, a sports psychologist, offers psychological insights about those who jump.

The second section—the poetry and science fiction—seeks to explain the mystique, the hypnotic fascination of skydiving. Consider the poetry: James Dickey's "Falling," an evocative, epic poem of what it might be like to *fall* out of an airliner in flight, to Steve Osterlund's "First Flight," to Charles Ghigna's "Divers," an award-winning poem. These all explore the world of flying and jumping. jeanni McCombs and George McCulloch see the sport differently, and Jim Rogers offers a rollicking Paul Bunyanesque-tall tale, "The Phantom Tenth Man." Each exceptional, each a different jump, if you will.

Lori Spring's science fiction piece, "The Eternal Skydiver," poses the question: what would happen if a sky diver made a high altitude jump *as the world was ending?* It is as haunting as the old tale of "The Flying Dutchman" on his eternal quest . . .

The third major section portrays the leaders in the sport: men and women (no chauvinism here) young and old, the people who contribute their time, efforts, their *lives* to our sport. These, I suggest, are some of our finest examples: Al Krueger; The Golden Knights; Joe Kittinger; the "novice"; Jerry Rouillard, jeanni McCombs; and George and Harriet McCulloch.

Finally, jump stories, dirt dives, hanger jumping: we all know it—when it's too windy to jump, we all hang around the DZ and tell each other war stories, jump stories, and outright lies. Each jumper in the sport has as many good jump stories as he has jumps in his logbook.

It is appropriate, I think, to end with Dean Frazier's

Preface xi

"Make a Skydive!," for ultimately, Dean tells us what some of us have forgotten about jumping—the basics, the joy, the sounds, the colors, and sensations.

Throughout the entire book, you will enjoy Ray Cottingham's free-fall photography. His work illustrates a wide variety of skydiving experiences, large-size star work, point-of-view shots as the jumper flies in a star and all the fascinating images that an exceptional sky diver (Cottingham long ago won his Gold Wings for his 1,000th jump) and photographer can capture.

The author is grateful to those who contributed by-lined articles and poetry to this work. The United States Parachute Association also unhesitatingly offered help and facts and information during the completion of this book; my wife Jean sat patiently at a number of dropzones while I put on gear for "just one more jump. . ."

If you have not yet made your first jump, I hope this book shows the love, the mystique, the *addiction* of skydiving. If you are already a jumper, you know this. If you're a jumper, read this book when it's too windy to jump. Or when you're broke. If you have blue skies, do as Dean Frazier urges. . .

Make a Skydive!

Acknowledgments

Grateful acknowledgment is made to the following for permission to reprint previously published material:

"The Man Who Flew Like a Bat" by Martin Caidin previously appeared in *Barnstorming* (New York: Duell, Sloan and Pearce, 1965) and is reprinted with permission of Martin Caidin.

Selections from *The Long, Lonely Leap* by Joseph W. Kittinger and Martin Caidin (New York: E. P. Dutton Co., 1961) reprinted with permission of Martin Caidin.

"A MAD Look at Skydiving" copyright © 1967 by E. C. Publications, Inc. Reprinted by permission of *MAD* Magazine.

"Falling," copyright © 1967 by James Dickey (first published in *The New Yorker*), from *Self-Interviews*. Used by permission of Doubleday & Co., Inc.

"Stimulus Addition: The Sweet Psychic Jolt of Danger" by Bruce C. Ogilvie reprinted from *Psychology Today* Magazine. Copyright © 1974 Ziff-Davis Publishing Company.

"Peak Experience at 6:45 A.M." by Michael Horan copyright © 1975 by Michael Horan. Reprinted with permission.

The chapter "The First Jump Experience" originally appeared in slightly different form as "Eternity Above, Eternity Below" in *Dude* magazine. Reprinted by permission of Dugent Publications, Inc.

The chapter "The George and Harriet McCulloch Story" originally appeared in slightly different form as "No Sky Too High" in *Parachutist* magazine. Reprinted by permission of *Parachutist* magazine.

"The Phantom Tenth Man" reprinted with permission of Jim Rogers.

"The Eternal Sky Diver" by Lori Spring reprinted with permission of *Skydiver* magazine, Lyle Cameron, editor.

"Make a Skydive" reprinted with permission of Dean Frazier.

The author is grateful to Steve Rossetti for guidance and advice during the completion of this book.

*Author and skydiver Steve Rossetti
suggests several answers
to the oldest and most frequent question
ever asked of sky divers . . .*

Why Jump Out of a Perfectly Good Airplane?

by Steve Rossetti

The first question a sky diver hears when someone finds out he's a jumper is, "Why do you jump out of perfectly good airplanes?" Jumpers are so sick of hearing this question that they never give it a straight answer. Many have their own flippant response such as "Why not?" or "If you were in those ratty old planes we use, you'd jump too."

These types of answers are normally sufficient since the question was only asked in a rhetorical manner. What the person really meant to say was, "you're an idiot for jumping out of airplanes; you'd never catch me doing such a stupid thing." Both walk away from the exchange feeling they had the upper hand. The non-jumper congratulates himself for exposing a mentally-warped person in such an eloquent manner. The jumper, on the other hand, figures the other person too dull-witted to experience spiritual enlightenment and refuses to waste a good jump story on him. The game of verbal volleyball then ceases for the moment, to be re-enacted time and again.

But if a jumper stays in the sport long enough, he will inevitably ask himself the very same question, "Why *do* people jump out of airplanes?" The gut reaction of any budding scholar to this question is that there are as many different reasons as there are people. No one can doubt the wisdom of such a response, but a closer scrutiny of the problem would reveal that there are certain common threads of thought that run through jumpers' minds when they decide to hurl their bodies at the ground.

The most obvious reason that first appears to any parachute instructor is that of *curiosity*. His Saturday morning jump classes are filled with a lot of wide-eyed students who can't wait to find out what it's like to take that long step out of the airplane door. Many of them also want to be able to say they've done it. It makes marvelous conversation at a cocktail party and allows one to put a notch in his belt signifying another experience added to the list. They are the world's professional amateurs and are the first to exit the sport, usually after their first jump. The curious and the experience-seekers make up the bulk of any class and it's a fortunate instructor who has one-third of his students return to the drop zone to make their second jump.

Some of those that stick around to try a replay of their first jump are the "thrill seekers." Skydiving more than satisfies their needs, at least in the beginning. Few sports can compete with the rush of the wind when the jump door is open, the excitement of stepping out into the void, and the tense moments watching your parachute open. A jumper never completely loses those heart-in-the-mouth sensations regardless of how many jumps he has. Like any new found thrill, though, a certain callousness does eventually develop and the thrill seekers, while still getting high over each jump (excuse the poor pun), are unsatisfied and look for bigger kicks elsewhere. They soon join the "curious" in the ranks of the ex-jumpers.

Still left in the sport are the "macho" types who place skydiving in the same category as car racing, climbing mountains, and wrestling alligators. No one can doubt that jumping out of an airplane takes a bit of courage and the macho types stretch the sensational part to the limit. They're an easy breed to spot at the drop zone. They're the ones who pull their ripcords at the last possible moment, hoping to "wow" the crowd. The bigger the crowd, the more spectacular the performance of aerial deftness and brilliant canopy work. Some of them leave the sport when they realize the size of the crowds around an average drop zone is not worth breaking their necks for. Or, they leave when their friends get

Why Jump Out of a Perfectly Good Airplane? xvii

tired of hearing tales of how they narrowly escaped death for the 105th time. A few exhibit too much macho and end up killing themselves. Still a couple of machos do stay and mill around drop zones. They spend most of their time talking about jumping and doing very little of it. They are the sport's "hangar jumpers"; they rarely get outside the hangar.

Then there's a sort of "Peter Pan" mentality in many sky divers. By jumping out of airplanes they seem to be saying, "I won't grow up—I don't wanna go to school." They reject middle class America and its cares and responsibilities. They too can fly—and in this fairyland, death has no power. The jumper flaunts death and its worldly counterpart—an urbane life. As he leaves the airplane, the jumper enters a surrealistic realm and only upon reaching the ground does death once more become a reality and so too the mundane problems of the world.

But for those few brief moments, the jumper is in another world. Many of these Peter Pans stay in the sport, at least until their bubble is burst. Some get married; others find a "respectable" job, both find that their feet are now fairly rooted in the earth. A parachute jump has become, for them, unthinkable. The magic fairy dust is gone . . .

Perhaps, of the original class of students, one in forty is left. A few continue on because they've found a home. Like the surfing cults so popular in the 50s and 60s, the sky divers have their own tightly knit community. They're a small band of hardcore jumpers that are scattered across the United States with pockets in other countries of the world such as Germany, England, France, and South Africa. They number several hundred to maybe a couple of thousand and they congregate several times a year at the big parachute meets like the Zephyr Hills Thanksgiving Meet, the U. S. National Championships, and the World Parachute Championships. And, like any sport, skydiving has its own informal hierarchy. The "skygods" lead the pack.

Few jumpers could not recognize the faces of Jerry Bird, Scotty Hamilton, Carl Boenish, Gene Thacker, Pat Works, Bill Ottley, Dan Poynter, Ned Luker, Lew Sanborn, and many others whose pictures appear regularly in parachute magazines.

And this cult is young. Most are between the ages of

18 and 35. Skydiving does have its exception in George McCulloch, a New Yorker who started jumping at 55 and at 74 has logged nearly 1,000 jumps and is still going strong. Not surprising is that on the whole, this young group shuns authority and discipline. Jumpers are noted for their independence and self-confidence. They would hardly consider it a compliment to be called a conformist and accordingly the unwritten rules of conduct in skydiving are few. You need be only open-minded, easy to get along with, and able to take care of yourself in the air and on the ground. Little else is criticized.

For most of those who stay, however, skydiving is a feeling of freedom that is hard to match. The poor pilot is encased in his noisy, metal machine, but the sky diver's place is with the air and the clouds. It's just about as close to being a bird as man can get. Once in free-fall, the jumper, though falling at over 120 m.p.h., has no sensation of falling, but rather feels like he's floating in the air with the wind rushing by him. It's a serene and beautifully quiet time. The man feels truly a part of nature. Under canopy, the silence continues as the jumper floats to the ground under his delicate parachute. Being alone with the sky and feeling a small part of a vast world, but, at the same time, the jumper is refreshingly alive and aware of his being.

Finally, all those who continue to jump find it just plain interesting and fun. There are plenty of parachute meets to keep the competitors busy polishing up their skills, hoping to win a slot on the U. S. team. The not-so-competitive jumpers enjoy a day in the sun with their friends and a few "fun jumps." They don't care whether they can perform the fastest free-fall formations or come the closest to a small disc on the ground. They come to enjoy themselves and skydiving with friends *is* enjoyable.

In the final analysis, the human animal is a complex creature. No one answer to the question of why one chooses to be a sky diver can be acceptable. Most of us started as the curious—wondering just what *would* that first jump be like. And, like Mr. Macho, we need little coaxing to get us to tell our favorite stories of how we came so close to death. Even the most seasoned leapers still get a thrill out of the rush of the wind during free-fall and the serenity of a quiet canopy ride. I, too, don't wish to grow up (at least not yet) and long to enjoy those carefree months in that fairy world.

But also present in all jumpers are the more nobler feelings of friendship and belonging. There, at the drop zones, are the jumpers' friends and it's always a pleasant day of camaraderie, rain or shine. And finally, no person can stay in skydiving without acquiring a strong sense of freedom and a concrete feeling of being alive that was somewhat hazy when they were so confined to the earth.

Jumpers like to be thought of as a different breed, a cut above the crowd. Some of them are. For those that are, it's because of a combination of all the noble and not-so-noble reasons men jump. What makes them different is that they are a bit more human, a bit more real than the mere mortals that know only the ways of the earth.

Discover the joys of soaring like an eagle;
know the serenity of an atmospheric cascade.
Come along and you will find
Eternity Above, Eternity Below...

The First Jump Experience

In his enormously successful allegory, Richard Bach talks about seagulls, individuality, achievement—and flying:

> Most gulls don't bother to learn more than the simplest facts of flight—how to get from shore to food and back again. For most gulls, it is not flying that matters, but eating. For this gull, though, it was not eating that mattered, but flight. More than anything else, Jonathan Livingston Seagull loved to fly.

I read *Jonathan Livingston Seagull* when it began to be a successful piece of popular psychology. But I didn't understand it until an early gray morning during April, 1973. At about seven a.m., weighted down with over forty pounds of coveralls, backpack, chest reserve and jump boots, I stepped off the edge of a Cessna 182, at 2,800 feet. I began falling into the cool morning air, hit the prop blast and then I knew. I understood it all.

I understood Richard Bach's love. I understood the bird Jonathan Livingston Seagull. I understood and felt my fear, which slowly dissolved into controllable anxiety. I understood the wind, the flying. I understood the power of flight, the joy, the beauty and the speed. I not only felt exhilaration, I felt time changing for me and perceptions... This is the way it happened:

Several days earlier, I read through the classified pages of *The New Times*, an "alternative lifestyle" newspaper, in my hometown of Syracuse, New York. My eye caught a small classified. "Those interested in making their first or second parachute jump, meet at 7:30 Thursday evening," and it gave a date and place and one man's name. The man was a college student, liaison between the Syracuse community and the Seneca Falls, New York Sport Parachute Club. A dozen of us met him, a dozen interested in what parachuting was all about. We met again in Syracuse the next night, Friday, April 12, to drive together to Seneca Falls, thirty-five miles away, between Syracuse and Rochester.

The Seneca Falls Sport Parachute Club consisted of one unimpressive corrugated shell hangar, two small airplanes, one which looked terribly unsafe. It looked like a battered air taxi, with sections in contrasting colors of aluminum and yellow, as if it had been ground-rolled on several occasions and put together on whim. The hangar smelled slightly musty. Scattered on the floors and on a long packing table were a variety of army surplus green nylon parachutes, in various stages of assembly. None looked very reliable. They looked as unreliable as the Cessna outside. No Smoking signs were stapled on almost every wall panel, a warning everyone heeded because of the fire risk to the parachutes.

Paul Campbell, the Instructor-Jumpmaster, at first gave me no more confidence. At twenty-four, Campbell looked less like a college student than most of the undergraduates surrounding me. I learned later that Campbell was a senior at Cornell University in Ithaca, New York.

About 8:30 Friday night, Campbell began the four-hour training course required of all prospective jumpers. He began talking slowly about the Regulations, established by Federal Aviation Agency (FAA), the U. S. Parachute Association and the State of New York, which, among other things, forbade parachutists from dropping into cities without prior approval. "That's not for your protection," Campbell said, wryly, "that's so no one will hurt poor defenseless buildings."

No one laughed. The idea of falling into the middle of metropolitan Syracuse or Rochester was beyond my comprehension. I tried to visualize what it'd be like to parachute into midtown Manhattan and I couldn't form a picture in my mind. I couldn't even visualize jumping into Central Park.

The First Jump Experience

Campbell talked about aircraft procedures: who sat where in the plane; what the duties of the Jumpmaster and the pilot were; what emergencies could take place inside the airplane (a pulled ripcord, for instance, causing the parachute to inflate and perhaps blow out the side of the airplane, sucking out the door, parachutist and all); and what the rules of airplane traffic were, on the runway and in the air. Several learners, I could see, were daydreaming during Campbell's speech.

He mentioned the exit, the arch and the count procedures and quickly brought everyone's attention back. "When you are inside the plane," he explained, "the first man out will sit with his back to the instrument panel. You'll be seated on the floor of the plane, beside the pilot. I'll be your Jumpmaster and I'll be kneeling on—and between—your outstretched legs. I'll open the door and spot—locate the field and maneuver the plane into the right heading and right location for your exit. When I say 'Get your leg out,' you slide your left leg out of the door and notch your heel into the leading edge of the step you'll find outside the door. When I say 'Get Out,' you grab the door with the other hand, turn and pull yourself out of the plane, facing forward. Stand on that step with your right leg dangling behind you. My last command will be 'Go!' and when I yell that, you jump back, spring back off that strut and into your arch and count."

The standard arch, for beginning parachutists is a strained, bent-back, arms-and-legs-outstretched X, which everyone should attain a split-second after stepping off the airplane strut. The X holds the parachutist in the wind and keeps him stabilized. Any arm or leg movement which cancels the arch means potential trouble for the parachutist—especially if he's a beginning student or inexperienced with free-fall. There is also trouble with the wind blast and the steady faster and faster fall, until the parachutist—in freefall—reaches about 125 m.p.h. This is terminal, the ultimate drop rate for humans.

The count which all beginning students learn is: "Arch One Thousand, Look (at the ripcord) One Thousand, Reach One Thousand, Pull One Thousand, Arch One Thousand, Look Up (at the deploying parachute) One Thousand, Arch One Thousand."

Later, the parachutist in free-fall can vary the count, take five seconds of delay or ten or as much as sixty seconds (or more) of delay before pulling the ripcord and watching his parachute deploy.

We walked outside into the dark and Campbell demonstrated the arch and the vault off the step into the air. We all took turns kneeling in the airplane and struggling to change positions, sitting with our backs against the bottom of the instrument panel, and then getting a leg out, making the awkward turn to face forward, holding the strut, and then arching backward into the air, or in this case onto the ground. "Don't worry about falling off that step, you'll be off of it in a second anyhow," Campbell said. No one laughed this time either. The next day I would be shown scratches and marks on the diagonal strut. "Fingernails. Claw marks," one cynical veteran said, "Those kids just don't want to leave that strut." Later I would see that was true.

Instruction continued inside, where everyone took turns being strapped into a training harness hung a good six feet off the floor. Slowly, over a period of two hours, it began to dawn on several students, including one terribly small girl, what they had gotten themselves into. The training harness was a regular parachute harness that hung free from the ceiling. Campbell strapped each of us into it. We had to stand on a ladder while Campbell stood on a stool. The straps are tightened across the chutist's chest, between his legs and over his shoulders. They are uncomfortably tight on the ground, but the tighter they are on the ground, the better they feel in the air. When Campbell got me strapped into the harness (I volunteered to be first), he jerked the ladder out from under my feet and I swung free, under the ceiling.

Campbell showed us where the Capewell releases are—the safety system to cut away the main parachute, in the event a canopy malfunctioned. Campbell cautioned, "There are two types of malfunction. The first is the total malfunction where nothing—absolutely nothing comes off your back. In that case, don't hesitate—pull that reserve ripcord immediately. *Immediately!* There's an old saying in parachuting—*when in doubt, whip it out!* Get that reserve over you. If you have a partial malfunction, which happens more often, you have to cut away. If the main parachute has a 'streamer'—

The First Jump Experience 5

Jumper closing into slot at sunset (Ray Cottingham photo)

that is, it unfolds, but doesn't deploy—pull your Capewells and your reserve ripcord."

The Capewells are two covered rings on the shoulder straps. (You flip the covers down and two wire rings appear. You pull each ring with a thumb and that pops the main parachute lines away from the harness. Then you pull your reserve ripcord.)

Campbell ordered me to run through the procedure in the harness. I got the Capewells uncovered, hooked a thumb into each and pulled. Instantly I dropped two feet headfirst toward the floor. The Capewells released and only another set of lines kept me from hitting the floor.

"See?" said Campbell, smiling just a bit, "you have to be fast. You gotta get that reserve out. Whip it out!" He brought the ladder back, worked me back in the Capewells and hung me again into the harness. He ordered me to go through the procedure again. This time I barely got one hand on the reserve ripcord—again didn't get it out—before I dropped toward the ground.

"What ya gonna do if that happens at two thousand

feet?" said Campbell. I began listening to him with greater reverence. I later found out what would happen. In his book, *Parachutes and Parachuting,* Bud Sellick writes:

> Those of us who began experimenting with maneuvers in freefall before establishing positions were discovered had great fun plunging out and assuming certain positions just to see what happened. Completely uncontrolled fall is exciting when recovery to stable fall is always within immediate reach, but uncontrolled fall is sheer terror when recovery is not within the jumper's grasp. Clawing a ripcord from its pocket while in chaotic tumbles or spines, I've see that glob of unsheathed canopy shoot past my legs, trailed by a writing mass of tangled lines. In those split second lifetimes I've heard myself screaming warnings from some detached point in time and space, and when somehow all the lines clear themselves and the canopy blasts open, the shock jolts me back to reality. I am no longer viewing experience from some remote vantage point, but am a flesh-and-blood participant. Often a tiny trickle of blood verifies this truth, where a buckle digs into a shoulder or a connector link grazes the ear.

Campbell continued, "Another malfunction is typically called a Mae West. If the main parachute lines get tangled, the parachutist may look up to check his opened rig and discover the two bra-shaped mounds instead of one smooth cone. The procedure is the same if that happens. Pop those Capewells and pull that reserve. Although some have chanced it in the past, you can't ride a Mae West to the ground because the falling speed is far greater than normal and there is no control over the chute.

"If you drift toward power lines, concrete, rivers, lakes or other potentially deadly spots, a Mae West can't be guided away from them. You have to trust the wind to blow you to safety. All parachutists have steerable reserve chutes, which are a damn sight better to ride down than a malfunctioning main chute."

I was unstrapped and let down out of the training harness. Over the next hour or so, I had a chance to watch everyone else worry through their experiences with their Capewells, counting, and arch. Many forgot the arch and count entirely. Campbell made them do it over. One small coed slowly became more and more terrified of the whole experience, until she simply cowered in a corner like a whipped puppy.

Only two of the twelve students were able to move quickly enough to jerk the ripcord away from the reserve chute before dropping the two feet and swinging in the harness.

Campbell explained the rules for canopy control—how two small toggle lines, one on each side of the lines up from the shoulder harness to the parachute (called "risers") controlled side-to-side movement and, to a lesser extent with the surplus army parachutes, a drop on an angle, to the right or left of the wind line. Custom-designed sport canopies can "crab" amazingly well from side to side and can literally fly circles around a surplus "rag" parachute.

Campbell finally showed us how to fall—knees bent, elbows in, relax, fall to one side or another, take the shock with legs, sides, shoulders. "Don't fall on your ass—it hurts like hell. Keep your legs under you and fall on your legs." Pulling your legs up and taking the shock on your ass is called, logically enough, a "butt-strike," and immediately the parachutist thinks: "I've broken my ass . . . I've broken my back . . . I'm paralyzed . . . I'm dying . . ." although usually just such an injury is not serious. Most parachuting injuries are at ground contact—strained or sprained wrists, ankles, broken bones happen occasionally, but usually injuries are cuts and bruises.

After the class was over and most students headed for the nearest tavern, I offered Campbell a beer and asked him to talk about parachuting, skydiving and himself. My collegiate-looking instructor had almost two hundred jumps, had qualified with a U. S. Parachuting rating of "C" (the ratings, from beginners to expert are labeled "A", "B," "C," and "D").

I popped open beers for the two of us and Campbell began talking about his own parachuting experience. "I began jumping in January, 1973. I wanted to see what it was like and my first jump was in the winter . . . it was ten degrees below zero out there when I jumped. I didn't know it was that cold. I was really charged up. The adrenaline flowed through me and when that door opened, I got out there—bang—I was really charged up about getting out there.

"I had to pop off a malfunctioning chute during my sixth jump—my first free-fall jump. I had a premonition that something would happen and it did. I had a Mae West and popped those Capewells. With over 170 jumps, I've only had malfunctions twice—which isn't bad at all.

"I know guys who have jumped 400 times with no malfunctions. In free-fall, when you have to pull your own ripcord, you have to learn to get steady in the air, to hold that arch. After you reach that point, you have other problems to overcome . . . how not to slip backwards or slide off sideways, and not to tuck your head down and dive like a bomb. If you slip off your arch and fall out of control, all you have to do to recover is arch and hold it—the arch will pull you right-side up again, automatically. After about fifteen jumps, everyone learns how to fall and when to pull the ripcord," (which isn't cord or rope at all, but unbreakable steel cable).

After his thirtieth jump, Campbell began to use advanced parachutes, first a Para-Commander, then a Para-Sled*, which looks like an inflated, floating waterbed.

"The sled is unbelieveable," he says and his eyes sparkle when he talks about it. "Your 'rag' has a five-mile-an-hour forward speed. My sled runs at twenty-five miles per hour and banks like an airplane. Someone once said that in the air, a good parachutist can do anything an airplane can, except go up. That's right. I can fly rings around 'most any other chute in the sky.'"

I asked about courage—if parachutists had a higher courage level than most people. "I don't think so," Campbell said, thoughtfully sipping his beer. " I know people here who aren't very courageous. They do have a high safety awareness. Every time I go up, I momentarily touch my Capewells and remember what they're for. We're not like that TV show 'Thrillseekers.' We believe the more you know, the less trouble you'll have in the air. We don't hide the fatalities, but we don't dwell on them either. Actually, there aren't that many . . ."

---

* Since this chapter was first written, the Para-Sled has been succeeded by other, better, square canopies, including the Strato-Star, ParaFoil, StratoCloud, Strato-Flyer, Viking, and Cruisair, among others. A square reserve canopy, the Safety-Flyer, has also been commercially available. By the late 1970s, the Para-Sled has become only a curiosity.

Twin Beech exit with sunburst (Ray Cottingham photo)

There aren't. You can get into more trouble on your local expressway than you can in the air. According to the U. S. Parachute Association, there were 35 deaths in 1972, and 1968 through 1972, the highest accident year was 1969, when 37 jumpers were killed. Many of these deaths could have been prevented with the use of a Sentinel, which would automatically open the reserve chute (one recent death occurred when a man died of a heart attack in free-fall).

Campbell and I popped open more beer as he kept talking. "After students take their first five jumps and are okayed for free-fall jumps—when they pull their own ripcord—then they have to start packing their own parachutes. It's complicated and takes time at first, but after a while, they learn how to fold—'flake'—the parachute, stow the lines, 'S'—fold it into the pack and fold up the pack. The curse of every parachutist is that he has to re-pack his own equipment. Now, I can pack a rag chute in ten minutes. My sled takes a bit longer to pack. You have to remember—the neater it all goes into the pack, the neater it all comes out. And almost every chute deploys and inflates less than two seconds after that ripcord is pulled . . ."

Campbell has taught "well over 100 students" and put that many out on the airplane step and into the air.

Had he ever had students chicken out and get back into the plane once they got out on the step, at say, 2,800 feet? "Nope, if they get out on that step, they're going baby. I have never kicked anyone, but they go off that step. I've had people hold on to the strut, but they don't hold long if they step off that strut. The air speed is too fast for them to hold on."

Had anyone ever tangled the lines on the way down? "Sure," Campbell says, "One kid on his first static line jump fell head down. I Jumpmastered him and as he fell, I short-lined him—I pulled up on his static line and when the chute opened, he was yanked right side up and had a successful jump from then on . . ."

Well past midnight, and after the rigorous four-hour course, I had trouble thinking about what Campbell was telling me about high altitude parachuting. I couldn't comprehend it.

What's the best thing a beginning parachutist should know? "Just relax. The parachute is one of the simplest things ever devised. Once you get confident this thing is going to open, time after time, once you can say to yourself, jeez, this thing works, then you can have a ball . . ."

At six a.m. Saturday morning, in the pre-dawn dark, I laced on jump boots and pulled on a ripped pair of coveralls. Campbell helped strap me into a "rag" parachute. David Misko, who holds a "C" license, checked everyone's packs, as did Howard Martin, principal owner of the drop zone. "Who wants to be first out?" Campbell asked.

"I do," I volunteered, not because I really did want to be first out, but I didn't want to have to watch others out there on that strut. "This plane looks like shit," I said, as walked toward the battered Cessna.

"See that other one?" Campbell asked, pointing to a beautiful blue and white Cessna, loaded with other students. "That one has been ground-rolled. This one, with all the multicolored sections, is fine. We're just repainting it."

Campbell, the pilot, two other students and I wedged into the Cessna. Campbell knelt across my legs, pinning me to the floor. After only several minutes, we got to 2,500 feet, then about 2,800 feet. My ears popped with the pressure. Campbell opened the door beside me and I couldn't have been more petrified. The wind pressure wanted to blow the door up against the bottom the wing. Campbell had to hold it down. Suddenly there was nothing beside me. Imagine your own car door blowing open at 85 m.p.h., on a mountain road, with a cliff edge beside you and you have an idea what it was like.

"Get a leg out," Campbell yelled. I did. "Get out!" I grabbled for the strut, clumsily, and pulled myself into the wind and onto the strut. I had to look down and was—if not terrified, close to it. I looked between my legs, down, down, down, down, 2,800 feet. I held on and edged away from the plane, along the step and daintily dangled my right foot behind me.

"Go, Go, Go," Campbell yelled.

I let go and pushed. I caught the prop blast, my helmet blew down over my eyes and as I reached up for it, I had fallen fifteen feet and the static line had opened my chute. I had no time for the arch or count.

I looked up and loved the parachute. The transparent green and white chute, which was dark green on the ground, was fully open.

I pulled the toggles, turned around and faced the airport. For the next two and one-half minutes, I floated down, down, down, over brilliant green fields, deep brown roads, and through magnificent blue sky. There is little sensation of falling—just drifting in the air. There is a peaceful stillness and a slight rocking to the chute.

I was not afraid. I loved the ride. I understood Jonathan Livingston Seagull. The rawest amateur, in a cheapo "rag" chute, I felt like an eagle. I understood the power, the speed, the grace of flying. I was alone. The other parachutists were behind and higher than I was. I had the morning sky to myself.

*　　　　　*　　　　　*

That beginning, multiplied thousands and thousands of times each year, throughout the country, and literally throughout the free world, shows student jumpers of all ages the silence, the thrill, yes, the anxiety, of that first jump. Many never take the second jump; they leave the parachute center—the "Drop Zone"—with an unforgettable experience and little desire to try it again.

But for those who do return—weekend after weekend, month after month—parachuting, and the expert high altitude skydiving, is addicting in the best sense of the word. For there is nothing—*nothing*—like stepping away from an airplane at 7,500 feet and sliding toward other sky divers to form a "star" a mile above the earth.

Skydiving is the fastest, most precise sport the human can indulge in without the benefit of machine surrounding him. Rocketing down through the sky, at upwards of 200 miles per hour, the sky diver rarely feels panic, often feels a surge of pure adrenalin.

And beginners taste only a fraction of what the sport offers.

Skydiving has been called the first sport of the space age. Throughout the rest of these pages, we'll try to show why . . .

*Sport champs who plunge from airplanes
or push a racing car to the limit
are fighting boredom by facing fear;
they aren't crazy.
The personality profiles
of over 250 risk takers reveal
people with a strong sense of reality
and a high degree of emotional control.
Smart, too.*

Stimulus Addiction: The Sweet Psychic Jolt of Danger

by Bruce C. Ogilvie

Protected by little more than their own skins, many athletes confront death and injury regularly. Skydiving from 12,000 feet or race driving at 180 miles an hour, these competitors eagerly seek situations that most people try to avoid.

Many of the athletes engaged in high-risk sports are stimulus addicts, people with a unique need for the special excitement found at the outer limits of physical and emotional endurance. After studying over 250 national and world class athletes, my colleagues and I find that for these people, risk is exhilarating, stimulating and sensual. A sky diver describes her first jump:

"There's a new sensation; it's not a sensation of falling because there's nothing to orient yourself with, no fixed thing to see falling that fast away from you. You don't get that pit-of-the-stomach feeling and it's just relaxing, like lying on a pillow of air. All you feel is the air against you, a slight pressure on your body, like lying on an air mattress."

Previous studies of risk takers assume that "emotionally healthy" individuals prefer security and safety. Those athletes who know the risks and choose to face them, therefore, must suffer from one or more mental pathologies such as:

- Counterphobic reactions, in which the individual repeatedly exposes himself to conditions or situations that at an

unconscious level provoke the greatest psychological or physical fears.
- Fear displacement, in which sports participation substitutes for an object or situation threatening the athlete.
- Supermasculinity, where overt behavior is the opposite of disguised, unconscious feelings of inadequacy.
- An unconscious death wish. This explanation, which is the one most frequently offered, presents risk taking as an attempt to gain temporary relief from a constantly nagging unconscious impulse to die.

After years of research at every level of competition from Pop Warner to pro, we find that all of the above explanations are true—some of the time. However, none of them are true enough of the time to represent accurately the risk-taking personality. Interpretive difficulties arise because the average spectator—including the psychiatrist—places himself in the athlete's parachute. While so suspended, he conjures up a wide range of negative images. A sky diver describes how: "The majority of people think you are crazy. How can you stand to do such a death-defying type of sport? My sister's is a typical response: It's really great, but the only reason it's great is because I've gone somewhere with it. I've competed internationally and I've gotten to travel. It's good to that point. But she still thinks that I am stupid, that I have no common sense."

Other, more positive interpretations conclude that by taking risks individuals impose on themselves the stresses that allow temporary escape from an over-protective society. Even these assessments tend to view risk-taking athletes as thrill seekers, frivolous by nature, who should find more worthy goals on which to risk their lives and bodies.

We collected psychological inventories on a group of athletes of national or world caliber. The purpose was to find out more about the personalities of those who mix fear and excitement to place themselves on the razor's edge.

Information came from tests, such as the Minnesota Multiphasic Personality Inventory (MMPI), the Edwards Personal Preference Schedule (EPPS), and the Cattell 16 Personality Factor (16PF), combined with tape-recorded interviews.

Jumpers exiting a Lockheed Loadstar (Ray Cottingham photo)

A dangerous mix. The sports represented spanned a spectrum from placid to perilous, with injury and death mixed in varying proportions. Of the thirty professional sports car drivers we studied in 1968, five have since died of racing accidents. Five others retired due to incapacitating injuries. Sixty percent of the All-Pro football players studied were no longer active five years later, many having retired due to injuries. Nationally, parachuting deaths ranged from twenty-three to forty-six in each of the last six years. Such risk-taking sports produce stress. Athletes studied were those who sought this stress through the years of preparation, training and competition required to become among the best in their sports.

At this uppermost competitive level, men and women share an almost identical personality structure, and we may confidently speak of the *human* tendency to seek risk. The need to prove one's manhood clearly does not explain the risk taking.

The sky diver's sister, who thought he must be stupid, also had the wrong explanation. Risk takers consistently excel in tests of abstract reasoning, where they are found to fall in the upper fifteen percent of the population.

Based on several measurements designed to reveal a person's desire for success and recognition, these stress-seeking individuals truly separate themselves from the average person. Their scores always place them in the upper quarter of the population, and on some measures in the upper five percent.

This desire to be on top combines with an inclination to be apart. These athletes are extremely autonomous people who definitely march to their own beat and have slight regard for the advice or counsel of others. Female race car drivers are the most independent athletes; pro-football players are the least autonomous.

Risk takers share a great will to dominate, seeing themselves as persons whom others trust and depend on. When there's a decision to be made, the risk taker assumes he will lead and that others will follow.

Several sections of the personality inventories combine to present a picture of people who are self-assertive and forthright. They make their own decisions and brook no interference from others. A sky diver, for instance, describes herself as, "Always very stubborn as far as getting my own way about things. I was always very domineering or bossy about almost everything. Those things maybe were more emphasized when I found something I could excel in and when I got enjoyment from something in a sport."

Alone and Apart. Risk takers are loners. All the groups tested were consistently above average in a cluster of traits which suggest emotional detachment from others. The sole exception to this profile of a reserved personality is the pro-football player, who is significantly more warm-hearted and outgoing than other risk takers, perhaps an occupational necessity for a team player.

This emotional detachment also manifests itself as a reluctance to offer emotional support or counsel to others. Social workers they are not. Their favored relationships are transitory in nature, requiring only a superficial commitment; they neither seek nor encourage deep emotional ties with others. A typical self-description is that of one female sky diver: "I try not to let people get really, really close to me. With the job I have and jumping, I don't make a lot of friends. I have a lot of acquaintances and I know a lot of people, but people that I really trust and feel like they are friends of mine are very few."

Past research suggested these risk seekers would need order and conformance to traditional morality. They would tenaciously pursue tasks and be unlikely to seek change. Instead, we found a decided trend toward disorganization, increased needs for nonconformity, rebellion against routine, and an essential desire for varied and different experiences. Social rebellion and a rather broad rejection of traditional standards suggest that these competitors are highly selective with respect to the social customs they choose to honor.

Findings from the MMPI are of particular interest, since this test was designed to identify the type of mental pathology that others attribute to risk takers. Studying the interaction of the ten MMPI clinical scales, we find profiles of people with a very low level of anxiety, a strong sense of reality, and a high degree of emotional control. They are adaptable, resourceful and energetic, and are willing to take the consequences of their own behavior.

Neither emotional instability nor neuroticism increase as the risk associated with a particular sport rises. On the contrary, there is a decided trend toward greater emotional stability in race drivers and parachutists, where risk is most clearly present. These competitors rank at the highest level in abstract ability, creativity, independence, and leadership potential, while scoring extremely low in measures of anxiety.

Facing Fear. There is, similarly, no support for the view of risk taking as a flight from unconscious threat or fear. In an interview shortly before the crash that took his life, race driver Ken Miles talked about the dangers of his trade: "You're extremely conscious of accidents. You see your friends killed. You see the mistakes they make and you try to protect yourself against those mistakes. The races you don't finish, you don't win. Nobody is absolutely perfect, and every so many hundreds of hours you're going to make a mistake which you can't recover from. If you can't alleviate the effects of the accident, you may get hurt, but this is part of the game. You're bound to have one every so often—you can't help it. I didn't get all this gray hair for nothing in 47 years, without being careful. It's easy to die young if you want to. I have no ambition to die young at all." Every driver and parachutist willingly and openly discussed the risks of their sport, often just before competing.

Certainly there are athletes whose basic motives could be labeled counterphobic, unconscious death wishes or some other unhealthy form of sublimation or compensation.

As a group, however, risk-taking athletes have a definitely positive personality organization. They are simply "stimulus addictive", that is, they have a periodic need for extending themselves to the absolute physical, emotional and intellectual limits in order to escape from the tensionless state associated with everyday living.

Like most humans, risk takers need stimulation and excitement. For them there is a special form of psychic ecstasy found by living on the brink of danger.

Perhaps risk taking will remain forever incomprehensible to the passive onlooker. Asked his motive for climbing Mt. Everest, Edmund Hillary replied, "If you have to ask the question, you will never understand why." A parachutist explained to me. "The adrenalin really runs. It's not because I'm scared. It's because I dig it."

*It started with Icarus,
daVinci and the rest. This is . . .*

The History of Sport Parachuting and Skydiving

Ever since Icarus dared the sun by flying on wings of feathers and wax and fell to his death when the wax melted, people have dreamed of flying, of coasting through the clouds and skimming over the ground like the birds. The advent of sport parachuting and another space age sport, hang gliding, has finally brought humanity as close as possible to the age-old dream of powerless flight.

In the middle ages, Leonardo daVinci is supposed to have dreamed the same dream and sketched a semi-rigid parachute, pyramid-shaped, with lines descending from the corners of the base. Whether he ever made a prototype remains uncertain, but there does exist a drawing of a device which looks remarkably like a parachute, squared off at the corners . . .

The history of modern parachuting has closely followed the development of powered flying. Credit for promotion and development of parachuting in the United States belongs in part to one woman, Georgia "Tiny" Broadwick.

The early 1900s were the time of early barnstormers, and when parachutes began to be manufactured, parachutists became as prevalent as flying barnstormers. In the minds of some, to this day, the term "barnstormer" and "parachutist" are synonymous. In his book *Sport Parachuting*, Charles W. Ryan cites the date 1908 as Tiny Broadwick's first parachute jump, a static line jump from a balloon over Raleigh, North Carolina when she was 15.

On June 21, 1913, she became the first woman to jump from an airplane and on August 7, 1913, she became the first person to make a jump from a "hydro-plane" piloted by Glenn L. Martin over the waters of Lake Michigan. She released herself from a trap seat at 2,000 feet. Ryan writes that her first free-fall jump developed because she became entangled in the tail of an aircraft in 1914, jumping at San Diego. She cut away from the entanglement with a knife and pulled what was left of the static line in free-fall, thus making by accident, the world's first free-fall jump.

Literature on the history of parachuting has often credited the first free-fall jump to Leslie Irvin, who is supposed to have made the first official jump in 1915. Tiny Broadwick, who made 1,100 jumps during her career, was later given honorary "Gold Wings" by the United States Parachute Association for her work in popularizing early parachuting. Once before her death, she scoffed at the idea of anyone paying for parachuting. "Someone always paid *me* for mine (jumps)," she is reported to have said.

The static line worn by Tiny Broadwick early in this century remained unchanged in design for years. The static line would play out as the jumper fell from the aircraft. When the static line tightened, the pack cover would rip open, pulling out the canopy.

The free-fall parachute harness and container is largely the same system: in free-fall, the parachutist pulls his ripcord, a steel cable pulls pins out of locking cones on the backpack, and a spring-loaded pilot chute pops out. The weight of the jumper falling against the pull of the pilot chute pulls the main canopy out of the pack.

About the time Tiny Broadwick was making her jumps, parachutes and parachuting became products for military development. During World War One, pilots began to take pistols with them and began firing random shots at enemy pilots during passes back and forth between the lines. Pistols led to larger guns and rifles (carried most awkwardly in biplane cockpits), and they led eventually to synchronized machine guns, firing between the blades of the aircraft propellers.

The History of Sport Parachuting and Skydiving

3 ParaCommanders landing (Ray Cottingham photo)

The first action to save the lives of pilots shot down was not an Allied innovation, but an Axis invention. A German pilot, shot down between the lines, drifted under canopy into Allied territory and the Allied staff was able to inspect and evaluate the worth of the German parachute.

Yet with almost every life-saving invention, there was a certain skepticism. Allied flyers vowed to stay with their burning, plunging aircraft, to needless death in a crash.

Parachutes were said to be risky and most Allied flyers shunned the bulky, unwieldy seat-pack parachutes. Pilots were sure that no one could breathe in a free-fall (a common idea among spectators today) and were equally sure that the free-fall itself would disorient anyone sufficiently to prevent quick deployment of the parachute.

Only a few courageous pioneers believed otherwise.

In the spring of 1919, at McCook Field, Dayton, Ohio (now Wright-Patterson Air Force Base), Leslie Irvin jumped from a Dehavilland DH-9 biplane at 1,500 feet. He fell in free-fall for 500 feet and pulled his ripcord . . . his pilot chute blossomed, the main came out and Irvin drifted to earth under a perfect canopy . . . and promptly broke his ankle upon impact. Irvin was excited with the parachute system — landing techniques could come later. Several days later, Floyd Smith also demonstrated the backpack free-fall parachute system without injuring himself.

Leslie Irvin later received the first order for mass-produced parachutes, an order for 300 for Army testing. Between World Wars, parachutes continued to be analyzed by the military for a variety of uses. In the cover article for *Life* magazine of March 22, 1937, "Aviators of 38 Nations Do Their Jumping in U. S. Parachutes," *Life* reported: "Today, Irvin Air Chutes are standard equipment for not only the U. S. Army, Navy and Marine Air Corps, but also for the British Air Ministry, Russia, Spain, Japan, Chile, Brazil and 30 other countries. Irvin parachutes are also used in commercial, air mail, and airline systems all over the world." The article also showed that parachutes had nearly doubled in price since 1938: "Last year (1937), Irvin used 125,500 yards of silk and a ton of silk thread in filling its orders. Its peak production was 124 parachutes a week, each one worth about $350."

Life also accurately guessed the value of the parachute for the military: "Long recognized as leaders in this sport, Russia now offers a new twist to parachute jumping: employing it as a military maneuver. A squadron of planes flies over a theoretical enemy line and drops men and machine guns in parachutes. Landing, the 1,200 men quickly pick up their 150 guns, advance upon the enemy's rear. Still untested

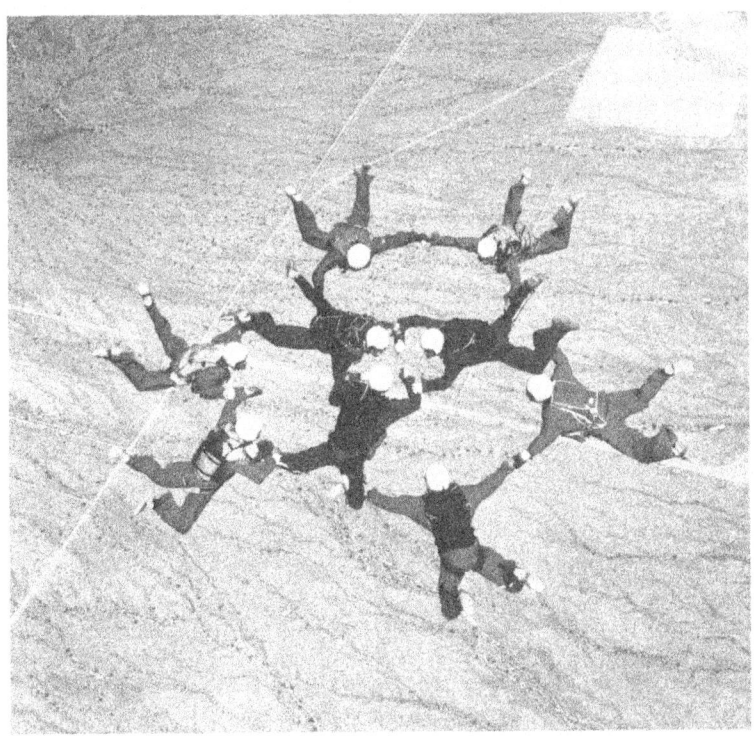

"9-man cluster" formation (Ray Cottingham photo)

in actual warfare, the strategem has definite offensive possibilities."

In the 1920s, General Billy Mitchell advocated the use of American military men as parachute troops. In 1928, he authorized a field exercise in which six troops jumped from a Martin bomber and set up a machine gun on the ground, a forerunner of the parachute troop concept.

By 1932, the sport of parachuting was beginning in the country as Joe Crane organized the National Parachute Jumpers Association, a forerunner of the Parachute Club of America, later renamed the United States Parachute Association.

By 1934, smoke jumping as a facet of the U. S. Forest Service had begun testing and organizing.

By the late 1930s, the sport and military use grew rapidly. The following is only a brief summary of the chronology of parachuting and skydiving:

1941: Arthur Starnes, a stunt jumper, skydived from 30,800 feet to 1,500 feet to prove that high altitude free-fall was physiologically possible.

1948: In Europe, Leo Valentin advocated the use of "bat-wings", semi-rigid wings which enabled a sky diver in free-fall to develop controlled free-fall body positions. The origins of the "track" and "delta" as skydiving maneuvers probably began during this period. The bat-wings, however, were inherently dangerous because air flow over the wings developed such force that the sky diver could not bend his arm to pull his ripcord. The wings were also unwieldly. Valentin was killed in 1956 in England making a demonstration jump when one of the "bat-wings" broke during his exit. He deployed both parachutes into a spinning malfunction and died in the impact.

1949: Sport skydiving began in France. Early leaders of American skydiving were Frenchmen such as Jacques Istel who spread the concept and methodology in the United States.

1951: The world's first international parachuting competition began when five nations met in Yugoslavia.

1954: The second World's Parachuting Championship was held in St. Yan, France. The United States was unofficially represented by one man, Army Seargeant Fred Mason, who competed against teams from eight European countries. Raymond Young, a French-American, wrote an article in *Flying* magazine, titled "Free-Falling French." He was the first to use the term "skydiving."

1955: Jacques Istel organized and trained the first U. S. Sport parachuting team.

1958-1960: The U. S. Army officially recognized and encouraged parachuting; the first commercial parachuting center opened at Orange, Massachusetts; Steve Snyder and Charles Hillard passed a baton to each other in free-fall, beginning the first aerobatic maneuvers which developed into Relative Work, and Captain Joseph Kittinger jumped from 102,800 feet to a deployment at 18,000 feet. (More about Kittinger on page 146.

1962: The first qualifying courses for parachuting

Instructor-Examiners were conducted by the Parachute Club of America.

1963: The first rules governing sport parachuting were established by the Federal Aviation Administration (FAA). Later, state and local governmental agencies would add other rules and, and in some cases, attempt to outlaw sport parachuting on a local basis.

1964: Introduction of the ParaCommander, the first truly modern sport parachute canopy. The PC was the sports car of parachutes until the early 1970s when the wing or ram-air parachute was first sold commercially. The PC spawned many imitators, including the Crossbow, Sparrow, Russian PC, Starlite and others. The first six-man "star" was formed over Arvin, California, opening the skies to larger and larger free-fall formations and giving the sport a new emphasis, that of Relative Work.

In terms of technology, there have been three major periods of innovation in the short history of American sport parachuting. They can be summarized as:

Late 1950s: Introduction of the line of Cessna 150-152 model civilian aircraft. Although the Cessna Company had been established since the late 1930s and had significant contracts for aircraft during the Second World War, post-war models were not extremely popular until 1956 when the 150-152 models were introduced. This would lead to the Cessna model 195, with a large radial engine, and later to the 180-182 models and the entire Skyline series. The various models of Cessna aircraft have proven to be the most accepted aircraft for small parachute centers. The various models of the Twin Beech aircraft have been the most successfully used larger aircraft, especially for eight- and ten-man RW jumps if the Beech is modified with a larger cargo door.

1964: Introduction of the ParaCommander canopy.

Early 1970s: Introduction of miniature equipment, such as the wrist-mounted altimeter as well as the introduction and general acceptance of the wing or ram-air parachutes, such as the ParaSled, ParaFoil, StratoStar, StratoCloud, Viking, StratoFlyer and Cruisair. The square parachute made the parachutist, for the first time, a *pilot* not just a captive of the winds. State-of-the-art progress grew dramatically during the decade of the 1970s, with the introduction of the single-point release system, such as the Booth Three Ring Circus and the adoption of the throw-away pilot chute, to replace the heavier and bulkier spring-loaded pilot chute. Along with the dynamic changes in technology, the art of Relative Work made 50-person (and more) free-fall formations possible.

Cheapos, PC's, downwinders & tracks--

The Language of Parachuting and Skydiving

Just like any other sport, skydiving has its own colorful and distinctive vocabulary. The following terms are in common use through the parachuting community, although your local *DZ* may well have its own variations. As new equipment enters the market, new terms arise *(Wonderhog, Three-Ring Circus)* and as older techniques become less popular *(Baton pass)* the language changes.

"A" License: Beginning license issued by the U. S. Parachute Association. For requirements, see the chapter on "Wings, Licenses and Ratings."

A.O.D.: Automatic Opening Device. A barometric- and speed-oriented mechanism that will automatically open the jumper's main parachute after a pre-determined number of seconds (CAP-3) or will automatically open the jumper's reserve parachute at a minimum safe altitude (Sentinel). BSR's suggest outfitting all novice jumpers with Sentinels on their reserves.

A.S.O.: Area Safety Officer, in charge of safety requirements and minimum safety standards for several area drop zones or clubs.

Accuracy: The art of free-fall jumping in which competitors aim for a target disc. Expert accuracy jumpers can hit the disc time after time; misses are usually measured in *cents* in competition. *Style* and *Accuracy* are slowly fading in popularity in favor of *RW* and *Sequential RW*.

Altimeter: Mechanical device that automatically gives the jumper a read-out of actual height above ground. Altimeters are getting smaller and smaller. They are now sold to fit on the wrist, strapped to the chest strap of most parachute harnesses, or worn on the top of a chest-mount reserve. Altimeters measure in thousands of feet or in meters.

Apex: The top of a parachute.

Arch and Count: Basic student learning technique and position. The arch prepares the student for free-fall and the count prepares him for a delay before opening his parachute. See "The First Jump Experience" for a longer description of the arch and count.

Assist pocket: A pocket built into the top of a *sleeve* which catches air during deployment and aids in proper deployment of the sleeve.

"B" License: Second license issued by the U.S.P.A. See the chapter on "Wings, Licenses and Ratings" for requirements.

B.S.R.s: Basic Safety Rules (Regulations). Rules, laws and guidelines issued by the F.A.A., U.S.P.A. and local officials governing jumping.

B 4, B 12: Surplus parachutes, modified for sport use.

Backloop: Back flip done in free-fall. Completion of backloops, front loops, and barrelrolls are requirement for the U.S.P.A. "C" license and are highly recommended for good RW jumping.

Backpack: The main parachute, worn on the back and the reserve on the chest, as opposed to the *piggyback* or *pigrig,* a tandem combination of the main and reserve, both worn on the back.

Bag deployment: Deployment of the main parachute from a bag, similar in size and shape to a knapsack, as opposed to a sleeve deployment. A bag will usually, although not always, allow a parachute to be packed smaller and tighter than a sleeve.

The Language of Parachuting and Skydiving

Barrelroll: Side roll, to the left or right, done in free-fall. Also a requirement for the class "C" license and good RW techniques.

Base: The "anchor" position in any relative work formation. The base is caught in free-fall *(pinned)* by the second, or pin jumper. A good base-and-pin combination is necessary to good fast stars. Without a stable base-pin the rest of the formation may be sacrificed.

Baton Pass: In the earliest days of RW jumping, a baton pass between two jumpers in free-fall was considered the ultimate achievement. Now no one bothers with this; everyone goes to four- or eight-man or larger stars.

Batwings: Rigid or semi-rigid extensions on the jumpsuit arms and legs. Because rigid batwings made it impossible for the jumper to bend his arm and pull his ripcord, batwings were judged suicidal and outlawed years ago. Not to be confused with underarm additions to the jumpsuit which are cloth and flexible.

Beech: Twin Beech aircraft. Beeches and other aircraft capable of carrying 8 or 10 or 12 jumpers (or more, in the case of aircraft like the SkyVan and the DC-3) made RW jumping possible.

Beer run: In many parachute clubs, the achievement of some individual goal: first free-fall, first two-man, SCR jump, first ride under a high performance canopy, or other achievement means that the participant buys beer for everyone. Sometimes beer to drink, sometimes beer to be showered over the jumper in question. Requirements vary with each parachute club. It's a rare jumper who hasn't had to buy beer for everyone sooner or later.

Bells: Jumpsuits with bell-bottomed sleeves and legs. The bells flare out in free-fall like the skin of a flying squirrel and allow the jumper greater capability for falling faster or slower and approaching a star with greater accuracy.

Blown Star: Free-fall star formation broken by a jumper who approaches the star too fast or too hard.

"Bomb Out". Unpoised exit out the door of a jumpplane. Mass exits during RW jumps are usually bomb outs.

Breakaway: See *Cutaway*.

Break-off altitude: The altitude at which time jumper abandons RW jumping and gets clear of each other for opening. With large stars (say 40 or 50) jumpers, break-off for some may well be as high as 5,000 feet.

Bungee: Heavy elastic bands which surround the container. When the sky diver pulls his or her ripcord, the pins and cones separate, the bungees pull the sides of the container apart and the pilot chute emerges to begin the deployment sequence. Spring-loaded pilot chutes would probably emerge without the aid of bungees, but most old-style backpacks employ two or three bungees to ensure the pilot chute emerges.

Butterfly snap: Wide, butterfly-shaped flange used to connect the chest reserve parachute to the main harness.

Butt strike: A classic fall in which the jumper hits the ground with—well, butt first—rather than feet first. May cause temporary injury to butt and spine, but is usually not serious. Jumpers who land with a butt strike in front of *whuffo's* usually injure their pride most of all.

"C" License: Third license issued by the U.S.P.A. See "Wings, Licenses and Ratings" for requirements.

C.S.O.: Club Safety Officer, who ensures safe jumping at a particular sport parachute club or drop zone.

Calendering: A process of treating fabric so that threads in the fabric are compressed and thus, less air gets through the fabric. A tighter weave results.

Canopy: The fabric. The umbrella. The parachute. Does not usually include lines, risers or capewells.

Canopy Assembly: The parachute, sleeve, pilot chute, lines, sleeve retainer line and sleeve. Everything ready to be packed into a container and harness.

Canopy R.W.: Relative work in which parachutists "fly" two or more canopies. The upper parachute of a two-man *canopy stack* may fly with his feet entwined in the top of the canopy below him. Usually, although not always, attempted with square parachutes. The coming technique of the future, according to many who fly squares.

Canopy release: Mechanism that will release a main parachute so that a parachutist may deploy a reserve. Formerly all metallic, although modern state-of-the-art releases may be velcroed fabric.

Capewell: Canopy release made by the Capewell Manufacturing Company. Generic term for all canopy releases is "capewell."

Caterpillar Club: Club for all pilots who had to make a parachute jump to save their own lives in early aircraft. Charles Lindbergh was a member. Presumably named because of the lowly caterpillar which produced the silk used for early (pre-World War Two) parachutes.

Center: A commercial parachute business that rents gear, sells supplies, offers the first jump course and offers aircraft for RW jumps. Comparable to a ski center.

Center Pull: Reserve parachute harness with the ripcord centered, neither on the jumper's left nor right.

"Cents": Centimeters away from dead center, a nearly perfect score in accuracy jumping, as in "I had a three-cent jump last time."

Cessna: Principal aircraft for jumping. Cessna aircraft make up 85 percent of the jump aircraft used for beginning and novice parachutists.

Chuting Up: The act of putting on and checking one's parachute gear prior to boarding the aircraft.

Clear-and-Pull: Five second (or less) free-fall delayed opening. Same as *Hop-and-Pop*.

Clock: Before general use of the altimeter, parachutists used a stopwatch to gauge time and height in free-fall. A jump from 12,500 to an opening point of 2,500 feet was a *60-second-jump*. Because of the clock-like face, altimeters are now often called *clocks*. Sky divers who formerly used both an altimeter and a stopwatch, now generally use only the altimeter.

Cloverleaf: Ripcord handle with general shape of three-leaf clover.

Cone: Cone-shaped piece of hardware, pierced to allow a pin to be inserted. The *pin-and-cone* lock the parachute pack closed. When the ripcord is pulled, the pins pull out of the cones, allowing the container to open and the sleeve or bag to emerge, thus beginning the development sequence.

Conference: Multi-state sub-division of the United States for administrative purposes, by the U. S. Parachute Association.

Conical: One type of reserve parachute, usually 26 feet in diameter.

Connector links: Metal hardware which connect the risers and the suspension lines.

Container: The part of the parachute pack which holds the parachute. The container is joined to the *harness,* which is fitted to the parachutist.

Controlled Air Space: The sky above Air Force bases, cities and other areas where parachuting is generally not allowed.

Control lines: Same as *steering lines.*

Conventional rig: Parachute system with an old-style, chest-mounted rig is considered conventional. New rigs are pigrigs.

Crabbing: Steering a parachute sideways to the wind for accuracy in landing. If the wind is north-to-south, the parachutist will crab by facing east or west.

Cross Connector links: A set of lines connecting the risers on some reserve parachutes.

Cross Pull: A ripcord which is across the body from the hand and arm used to pull; i.e., a cross pull for a right-handed parachutist would be a ripcord on his left side.

Crown lines: Lines across the apex of the ParaCommander or other similar parachute. Used to create tension during packing and help straighten the apex.

Cutaway: The act of activating the capewells to jettison a malfunctioning main parachute so a reserve may be deployed without opening into the main. The parachutists' first cutaway is usually an awesome and memorable occasion.

"D" License: The most advanced parachuting license. See "Wings, Licenses and Ratings" for requirements. Expert-level license.

D Rings: Metal rings, shaped like a letter "D" to which the chest-mounted reserve is attached.

DC-3: The Douglas workhorse of World War Two, still in operation on some drop zones.

DL-7: Specific modification in which the steering modifications look like the letter "L" (there are two) and are seven panels apart.

D.O. Jump: Delayed opening. Free-fall of 10 seconds or more.

DZ: Drop Zone. Where parachuting and skydiving is permitted.

Data Card: Card carried inside the reserve container providing the name of the owner, type of canopy, and particularly, when the reserve was last packed and by which rigger.

Dead in the air: A jumper without horizontal speed; one who is simply moving down. Can be compared to a stalled ship which is "dead in the water."

Delay: Any free-fall skydive in which the jumper opens his own parachute after leaving the jump plane. Delays are usually 10 seconds, 20 seconds, 30 seconds, 45 seconds, 60 seconds and over 60 seconds.

Delta: A free-fall body position in which the jumper's head and torso are lower than the legs. This allows the jumper to move diagonally downward and forward through the sky. RW jumpers who wish to become expert in their sport must master the *Delta* and *Track*.

Demo Jump: Any jump made off the usual drop zone, for spectators; usually at a county fair, circus, or other similar event. Only qualified jumpers can make Demo jumpers because of the added hazard of roads, power lines, buildings, spectators and other obstacles.

Deployment: The act of the canopy opening after the jumper pulls his or her ripcord.

Deployment bag: An alternative to the sleeve.

Dirt dive: Rehearsal by all jumpers of a planned RW jump on the ground at the DZ.

Disc: Target for accuracy jumpers.

Dive: A head-down position used to catch a star or other formation. Also refers to the *jump*.

Docking: The art of approaching a star and entering by breaking the grip of two jumpers previously in the star, and thus widening the circle, or completing the formation, if not a round star.

Door exit: Exiting the aircraft at the door, rather than on the strut.

Dope rope: See *static line*. Uncomplimentary term.

Downwind landing: Landing the parachute in the same direction as the wind is blowing will increase the parachutist's landing speed. Not usually recommended.

Dummy ripcord: Handle with a colored "flag" attached. Novice jumpers must make several good, precise dummy ripcord pulls before they can graduate to free-fall jumping. The dummy ripcord pull occurs when the parachutist is still on the static line.

Dump: To pull the ripcord and begin the development sequence, as in "I forgot where I was and dumped at 5,000 feet."

Exhibition jump: Same as *Demo jump*.

Exit: To leave the aircraft; may be either a *poised exit* or *bombout*.

Expert: Sky diver with a "C" or "D" license.

F.A.A.: *Federal Aviation Administration,* the arm of the U. S. government which controls skydiving, as well as sport and commercial aviation. Uncle Sam's representative at the local drop zone.

F.A.I.: *Federation Aeronautique Internationale,* international governing body which controls international skydiving, hang gliding, soaring and other sky sports. The U. S. Parachute Association licenses sky divers in this country on behalf of the F.A.I.

F.P.S.: Feet-per-second.

Field packing: Immediate rolling or stowing the canopy in the pack for the trip back to the DZ, in the case of a missed spot or for packing later, if the parachutist wishes to repack at home.

Flake: Verb and noun. To *flake a parachute* is to fold the panels for packing into the container, prior to jumping. A *flake* is a psychologically unreliable person to jump with. Most every DZ has its own local flakes.

Flare/flarepoint: Point at which the jumper ends a dive and raises his head to approach the formation.

Flat circular: Particular type of reserve canopy.

Flat spin: An uncontrolled spin, caused by inadequate body position and worsened by centrifugal force. Usually encountered by novice free-fall jumpers. If not stopped in time, can lead to blackouts and possible death.

Flat turn: Controlled turn. Jumpers in free-fall can turn left or right by using their shoulders, arms and legs like rudders.

Flight line: Where the jump-planes and other aircraft are fueled. No place to pack or dirt dive.

Floater: An RW jumper who, because of weight or jumping ability, exits *before* the base and pin (often by hanging on the edge or outside of the aircraft door) and *floats* (waits) for the base and pin to establish the beginning of the formation.

Flotation gear: Used when a DZ is dangerously close to a body of water deep enough to drown in. Flotation gear comes in a variety of sizes and shapes, but is usually kidney-shaped or basketball-sized inflatable balloons. Some jumpers believe that water gear that size is unreliable in keeping an adult afloat for any length of time.

Flyer: RW jumper who exits the aircraft last (or nearly last) and has to dive considerable distances to reach the base and pin, substantially lower than he was, on exit.

Frappe: To *go in*, a fatality.

Frappe hat: Lightweight leather hat worn by RW jumpers. Non-rigid. Officially not recommended for novice jumpers.

Free-fall jump: A delay of ten seconds or less. More than ten seconds is a *delayed opening* jump.

Frog: Basic body position in free-fall. The body is relaxed and this is a modified stable position. The frog is an accepted position for jumpers past the novice class. The head is slightly raised, chest slightly raised, arms bent at 45 degree angles.

May be tightened into more compact position for greater vertical descent. So-called because the basic position looks slightly like a frog at rest.

Front loop: Front flip in free-fall. Must be mastered for a class "C" license.

Funneled star: Star which breaks apart and falls into its own center.

Glide angle: The angle in which the parachute moves forward or the angle in which the parachutist approaches the target, in accuracy jumping.

Golden Knights: Nickname for the U. S. Army parachute exhibition team, headquartered at Fort Bragg, N.C.

Grip: Hold that the jumper has on another jumper to cement a formation. A *double grip* is a tandem grip by two jumpers on each others' arms, legs or torsos.

Hand track: A method of moving forward in the air by vectoring air with the arms and hands. Usually an ineffective way to build or sustain horizontal speed toward the objective.

Hard pull: Ripcord pull which takes more than normal effort (more than about 22 lbs. pressure). Packing problems usually account for hard pulls. A claim of a hard pull by a novice free-fall jumper is often attributable to unfamiliarity with the gear.

Harness: That part of the parachute system which the jumper tightens to form a cradle for his body. Usually the harness attaches at the chest, legs and lower belly. The F.A.A. issues regulations regarding the strength of webbing used in the harness. A tight but comfortable harness lessens opening shock; a loose harness distorts opening shock and may cause injury to the jumper, especially in the groin.

Hazards: Anything that can cause injury or death to the jumper. Notably, large and deep bodies of water, electrical wires and power lines, buildings and other obstructions, man-made and natural.

Helmet: Required by all jumpers. Many RW jumpers are using hockey helmets and frappe hats instead of the usual rigid motorcycle helmet. Old cliche and rule of thumb: if you have a $5 brain, use a $5 helmet.

The Language of Parachuting and Skydiving 37

Horrible malfunction under ParaCommander or PC-type parachute. This malfunction would not clear and must be cut away. Presumably the jumper came down on his or her reserve. (Ray Cottingham photo)

Hesitation: Deployment sequence slower than the usual one-and-one-half to three seconds. Hesitations are usually caused by the failure of the pilot chute to clear the jumper's back quickly enough.

High performance: Usually defined as a ram-air or "wing" type parachute. Rates of forward speed for the three basic chute types: rag chute or cheapo—up to 7 miles per hour forward; ParaCommander or PC-type—up to 17 m.p.h.; wing-type chute—23 m.p.h. and faster.

Hockey helmet: Used by RW jumpers, who think they get a better "feel of the air" with a lightweight helmet. Officially not recommended for novice jumpers.

Holding: Facing the wind, under canopy. If the prevailing wind is coming from the north at 10 m.p.h. and if the jumper is using a canopy with a "built-in" forward speed of 10 m.p.h., facing into the wind will give him a speed of zero. Thus he is "holding." Turning with the wind or *running*, would, in this case, give him a forward speed of 20 (wind speed plus built-in speed of the parachute).

Hop-and-Pop: Same as *Clear-and-Pull*. An exit and free-fall of less than ten seconds. Usually five seconds or under. The jumper *hops* off the step or door of the aircraft and *pops* open his parachute.

Hypoxia: Lightheadedness, giddiness, lack of motor control and reasoning ability caused by lack of oxygen to the brain. Jumpers above 12,000 feet (mean sea level) should be aware of the problems and potential dangers of hypoxia. The F.A.A. has set guidelines regarding use of oxygen at high altitudes.

Inboard Pull: Ripcord handle that is inside the left or right shoulder, rather than on the outside of the harness.

Instructor: Person who has passed all qualifying tests offered by the U. S. Parachute Association and is thus qualified to teach the first jump course and to instruct novice jumpers. See "Wings, Licenses and Ratings" for requirements.

Intermediate canopy: Paracommander or PC type parachute.

I/E: Instructor/Examiner. Qualified by the U.S.P.A. to certify instructors. See "Wings, Licenses and Ratings" for requirements.

Jumper: Informal slang for all sky divers.

Jumpmaster: Qualified leader in an aircraft full of static line or novice parachutists. The Jumpmaster will decide the jump run, coordinate it with the pilot, decide on the exit point and generally take command of the aircraft, subject to the flying decisions of the pilot. A *Jumpleader* acts as leader in an aircraft full of expert jumpers.

Jump Run: Straight and level flight at the correct altitude toward the exit point. The Jumpmaster may, during the jump run, offer course corrections to the pilot.

Keel Turn: A turn in free-fall using a leg as a fulcrum.

Kicker plate: An inexpensive aluminum 'pie dish' which is used to seat the reserve pilot chute. The kicker plate is jettisoned when the reserve is opened. Some jumpers with quick reflexes and even quicker presence of mind are said to be able to catch the kicker plate in mid-air as the reserve opens.

L/D (Lift to Drag) Ratio: The relationship between the lifting characteristics of the parachute as opposed to the resistance by air upon the forward speed of the canopy and the drag of gravity. Applied in generally the same way to airplanes.

Legal age: Usually 18 to parachute, but may vary by locality. Check with your local DZ.

Lift: An airplane load of parachutists, i.e., "I've signed up for the next Beech lift."

Line-Over: A malfunction in which one (or more) suspension lines has looped over the canopy.

Load: Generally same as *lift*.

Lobster Tail: Color combination seen on many ParaCommanders and other similar canopies. Front and side panels are one color, back panels a contrasting color, thus making the canopy appear like a lobster tail.

Logbook: Record book kept by all serious jumpers. The log will usually list all jumps in sequence, and has space for date of jump, location of the jump, aircraft type, jump type (static line, free-fall or delayed opening), altitude, delay in seconds, total free-fall time, distance from target, wind speed, parachute type, reserve type, maneuvers during jump (four-man RW, eight-man RW, etc.), comments and a space for a signature by a licensed parachutist, a Jumpmaster, or Instructor who witnessed the jump, or the jump pilot. New

RW logbooks have space to diagram each jump. Logbooks must be kept for licenses, qualification for 12- and 24-hour free-fall awards, 1,000 jump awards and other qualified and earned ratings.

Loft: Rigger's shop, where parachute repairs and sales are made. Lofts must maintain certain standards as required by the F.A.A.

MA-1: 36" spring-loaded pilot chute. Used on Para-Commander and other similar parachutes and on many standard backpacks. The new "throw-away pilot chutes" are rapidly replacing the spring-loaded pilot chute.

Mae West: Malfunction caused by a suspension line over the canopy. So-called because the parachute looks like a large bra, instead of like a round canopy.

Main: Principal canopy, as opposed to the reserve.

Malfunction: Any problem with the main canopy which may require a cutaway and deployment of the reserve. Malfunctions come in two types: a *total* malfunction occurs when the main parachute does not come off the jumper's back. Often called a *pack closure*. A *partial* malfunction may be either a *streamer*, which occurs when the sleeve deploys but the parachute does not emerge from the sleeve, or a *Mae West*. If the jumper has a total, he activates his reserve; if he has a partial, he does a cutaway, using his capewells and then activates his reserve. Failure to cutaway may mean that the reserve tangles with the partially open main above him, thus offering the jumper a nearly zero chance of safe recovery and descent.

Manifest: To sign up a complete load or lift of jumpers. Many jump centers require a complete manifest and tickets before jumpers can board the aircraft.

Mass Exit: In large-star RW, a nearly simultaneous exit, in which all the jumpers fall out the door like a line of dominos. Mass exits are an art; the best stars are put together when the mass exit is tight.

Modification: Any change in the basic characteristics of a parachute made by the factory or by a qualified rigger. Modifications may be a removal or change in a parachute panel, or change in the suspension or steering lines. Only qualified riggers and parachute factories are allowed to make major modifications. The F.A.A. has issued guidelines about which types of modifications may or may not be made outside the factory.

NB-6, NB-8: Surplus parachutes, Navy issue.

Night jump: Officially described as a parachute jump made from at least 5,500 feet one hour after official dark until one hour before official dawn.

Novice jumper: One who has made one or more parachute jumps but not yet qualified by a class "A" license.

O.D. Olive Drab. The color of most surplus parachutes (no one in his right mind would buy a *new* parachute in olive drab).

"On the Step": Novice static line or novice free-fall student poised on the step of a Cessna or other similar jump plane, ready for the "Go" from his Jumpmaster.

"On the Wrists": In a star and flying with other skygods.

Opening altitude: Altitude when the jumper should have a good canopy over his head. Usually this is 2,500 to 2,800 feet above ground level. Could be higher for mass jumps—large star attempts.

Open modifications: Modification not covered by mesh. Open modifications are potentially hazardous because a pilot chute may entangle through the modification and cause a partial malfunction.

Opening shock: The quick stop the jumper comes to when the parachute deploys fully. The velocity is from 120 m.p.h. at terminal to 10 m.p.h. within two or three seconds as the parachute opens. Opening shock used to be a major problem in military jumping, but since the advent of new generations of gear since the late 1940s and early 1950s, opening shock is no longer a real problem, although some jumpers are prone to complain about it. Faulty body position (head down) may lead to a hard opening shock when the harness flips the jumper into an upright position.

Outboard Pull: The ripcord handle under the left or right shoulder blade, but outside the edges of the webbing, rather than inside, over the jumper's chest.

Out-of-date: Reserve which needs to be repacked because it is past the deadline for legal use. U. S. Parachute Association members now need to repack every 120 days.

Oxygen: Needed for high altitude jumps. Consult your A.S.O. or drop zone operator for specifics in your locality. The F.A.A. sets guidelines for oxygen use by high altitude sky divers.

PC: ParaCommander: Since 1964, when it was first introduced, the ParaCommander has been the most popular and generally best received parachute in sport parachuting.

P.L.F.: Parachute Landing Fall. The best way to encounter the ground. The P.L.F. is taken with the legs together, knees bent, arms and hands in. The jumper is prepared to roll sideways (never straight forward onto his face or straight back, which may cause a whiplash). The jumper takes the ground shock on the side of his legs, side, shoulders, and does a complete roll, if necessary. The P.L.F. is elementary and necessary; the *stand-up* is a landing in which the jumper takes all the ground shock in his legs. It sometimes feels as if the jumper's knees are going through his spine and skull. The P.L.F. and stand-up are generally approved methods, the alternative is a *crash-and-burn*, in which the jumper encounters the ground with other parts of his or her anatomy, not at all gracefully and often painfully.

P.O.D.: Pack Opening Device. Similar to a *bag* system of packing and deployment.

Pack: Noun and verb. *The pack* is the jumper's complete parachute system; *to pack* is to flake and stow the parachute to make ready for jumping.

Packing: The act of flaking the parachute, stowing the lines and closing the container, to make the equipment jump-ready.

Packing card: See data card.

Packing mat: Protective canvas, plastic or other material used to protect the parachute from dirt, oil or anything else while packing on the ground.

Packing table: Protective table used when conditions are not suitable for packing on the ground. Some DZ's make packing tables from old diving boards, which are the right width; several dovetailed together will make a packing table the right length.

Panel: One portion of a parachute. Parachutes will have different shaped panels for different portions of the parachute.

"Pap": Short for Papillon, a French-designed parachute similar to the ParaCommander.

Parachute: From the French words *para* (to guard against) and *chute* (to fall); thus parachute means literally "to guard against a fall."

Parachutist: Jumper who has achieved a Class "A" license. Free-fall jumper. In the eyes of the public, *parachutist* and *daredevil* are still synonymous.

Pass: Straight and level flight at the right altitude toward the exit point. One aircraft may have multiple passes at various altitudes: "Give me one pass at 2,500, one at 4,500, and one at 7,500 on this lift," the Jumpmaster may say to the pilot.

"Peas": Target for accuracy jumpers usually made of *pea gravel*, plastic fiber, sawdust or other similar material.

"Pencil-packing": To repack a reserve parachute illegally by simply changing or adding a new "date of repack" to the data card.

Pigrig: Tandem main-reserve parachutes worn on the jumper's back. The Wonderhog and other similar systems are the latest "state-of-the-art" in pigrigs. The front reserve is quickly becoming passe in sport parachuting because of increased bulk and inferior flying characteristics.

Pilot chute: Small parachute that leaves the parachutist's container first. The jumper's weight pulling against the fully deployed pilot chute pulls the rest of the assembly out of the container and off the jumper's back. In England, the pilot chute is sometimes called the *Extractor* chute.

Pilot Error: In aviation, any crash, injury or fatality caused by mental lapses or mistakes on the part of the pilot. Many jumping injuries or fatalities are similarly caused by "pilot error" on the part of the jumper.

Pin: Noun and verb. *The pin* is a metallic prong which slips into the *cone*, to lock the parachute container closed until the parachutist pulls the ripcord. *To pin* is the act of catching the *base* jumper in free-fall to establish the *base-pin* section of a free-fall formation.

Pin-check: A last minute safety check performed before the parachutist boards the aircraft. Another jumper, a Jump-master or Instructor checks the complete main and reserve to see that the pins and cones are set properly; that the reserve is *in date;* that all latches are properly snapped and; in general, that the main and reserve parachutes are properly set for the jump. A pin-check will also include calibrating a Sentinel, if the parachutist wears one.

Poised Exit: An exit from the aircraft step or door in which the parachutist is ready seconds or minutes prior to the actual exit. Poised exits are required of novice jumpers, to learn correct positions and reactions. Later they graduate to *bombouts,* unpoised exits.

POPS: Organizations for "senior citizen" parachutists. Stands for *Parachutists Over Phorty.* Its insignia shows a worried Father Time, jumping in a rocking chair, pulling his ripcord with a walking cane, his fingers crossed for good luck. Membership is open to parachutists over Phorty—or, Forty.

Porosity: How much air can get through what kinds of material. Parachute fabric is classified low porosity or high porosity. *LoPo* parachutes generally will drop slower and let the jumper down softer.

Prop blast: Turbulence caused by the aircraft propellor. Jumpers often become unstable upon exit when they hit the prop blast or, as it is sometimes called, *prop wash.*

R'2s, R'3s: Non-metallic capewell-type releases.

Rag chute: Generic name for any surplus round parachute. Same as *cheapo.*

Railroad: To strike a free-fall jumper hard enough to cause possible injury, to destroy a formation or to knock a sky diver out of position. At the least, to railroad a fellow jumper is discourteous; it can cause a possible fatality if the jumper is knocked out and does not wear an automatic opener, such as a Sentinel.

Ram-air: New square type parachute. So-called because the air flows into the front of the parachute cells, and out the back; similar in concept to the intake and exhaust of a jet engine. Ram-air parachutes have the advantage of increased forward speed in the air (25-30 m.p.h.) but are also more difficult to handle and are generally regarded as the "sports cars" of the parachute world. Common ram-air parachutes are the StratoStar, StratoCloud, Cobra 10, ParaFoil, and others.

Relative Wind: An aviation concept, introduced to the world of skydiving by Pat Works in his book *The Art of Freefall RW*. Relative Wind is the wind which always comes at the jumper from the direction toward which he is moving.

Relative Work: See RW.

Re-pack cycle: The dates at which time the reserve parachute must be opened, checked and repacked. Repacking now is due every 120 days for U.S.P.A. members. For years, the re-pack cycle was 60 days.

Reserve: The parachutist's second parachute.

Rig: The parachutist's complete outfit, ready to jump. Same as *gear*.

Rigger: F.A.A. licensed parachute repairman and re-packer (in the case of reserves). Only riggers may repack reserves, and the rigger must sign the data card, giving his name, F.A.A. license number and the dates. *Junkyard riggers* are those who make repairs or equipment with spare parts or cheap equipment. A good rigger is your best friend when you need to use a reserve in the air. Many jumpers have been known to give their rigger a bottle of his or her favorite liquor when the reserve opens promptly as needed during a malfunction or cutaway. Needless to say, an inept rigger is nobody's friend.

Ripcord housing: Steel conduit that protects the ripcord.

Ripstop: Nylon that resists tearing. Ripstop nylon is also used for sailboat sails, as well as parachute fabric.

Risers: Webbing that begins at the capewells and extends over the jumper's head, where *suspension lines* are connected to the risers with *connector links*. Risers and most webbing on the parachute harness should withstand 5,000 pounds of pressure before splitting or breaking.

Running: The act of facing a parachute in the same direction the wind is blowing, for maximum advantage and speed. To run is to add the wind speed and the built-in forward speed of the parachute for maximum velocity. Opposite of *holding*.

R.W.: Relative work. To make a free-fall skydive with others; to jump relative to someone else. The act of completing (or attempting) a multi-person formation using hand-holding, or other physical connections to establish a formation in free-fall. Most jumpers believe that **R.W.** is the best part of skydiving. R.W. techniques have changed the face of sport parachuting. Only a few years ago, a baton pass between two jumpers in free-fall was considered expert jumping. Now R.W. techniques involve 50 (or more) jumpers connected in various "mega-formations." See Pat Works' *The Art of Freefall R.W.*

S.C.R.: Star Crest Recipient. The most respected and generally most sought-after earned award in skydiving. The S.C.R. is awarded to any member of an eight-man (or larger) free-fall formation held together for five seconds or 1,000 feet. Awarded by the Bob Buquor Memorial Star Crest Association.

S.C.S.: Like the S.C.R., but awarded to the eighth, or following jumpers in a free-fall formation. Stands for *Star Crest Soloist*.

Saddle: That portion of the harness on which the parachutist sits. A split-saddle harness is one with separate leg straps individually connected.

Sentinel: Automatic barometric- and speed-computer which will fire the parachutist's reserve open if the parachutist falls through the last 1,000 feet without having a good canopy over his head. The most popular automatic opening device in sport parachuting. Manufactured by S.S.E. Inc., Pennsauken, New Jersey.

Sequential RW: Relative work jump in which several different free-fall formations are completed. A four-man RW

Exiting two An-Z aircraft (Ray Cottingham photo)

team might go from a Skirmish line, to a four-man star, to a Murphy star during one jump, for instance.

Short-lining: In static line jumping, a Jumpmaster will *short-line* a static-line jumper by pulling in the static line to prevent the jumper from being entangled in the line or to begin the deployment sequence faster than normal. To *short-line a canopy* is to trim (shorten) the suspension lines to alter the flying characteristics of the parachute.

Shot bag: Weighted pouch used to hold down a parachute during packing.

Silk: What parachutes were made of before ripstop nylon. Pre-World War Two. The phase still remains, "Hit the Silk," a reference to early military paratroop jumping. Most modern jumpers have never even seen a silk parachute, much less jumped one.

Sitting Up: The jumper sits up in free-fall to stop. He literally raises his torso, arms and head.

Skirt: The bottom edge of a parachute canopy.

Skygod: Expert free-fall jumper, usually with an SCR, SCS or other RW experience and achievements. The skygod is sometimes a less-than-complimentary term, meaning a jumper who demands an ideal position on the load, or first lift, to the exclusion of others. An inconsiderate R.W. jumper, obsessed with his or her own perceived importance and abilities.

Sleeve: Long cloth protection for the canopy; the sleeve holds the canopy in the container and acts to slow the deployment sequence during opening. The sleeve also has room on the outside for stowing bands—rubber bands used to keep the suspension lines. In some containers and some systems, the sleeve has been replaced by the bag or P.O.D. (Pack Opening Device). The sleeve is one of the new innovations which make sport parachuting comfortable at opening shock time.

SL jump: Static line jump, in which the parachutist's canopy is pulled open by a static line, an unbreakable line which runs from the backpack to an anchor in the airframe of the aircraft. The novice graduates from an automatic static line to a self-actuated free-fall parachute rig.

Slots: Positions in an R.W. formation. *Near-side slots* are positions on the side of the formation nearest the aircraft; *far-side slots* are on the side of the formation opposite the aircraft. Far-side slots presume more *flying* ability on the part of RW jumpers to reach the other side.

Smoke: Noun and verb. Smoke, in the sense of a smoke grenade, worn on the boot, helps spectators locate a sky diver during a free-fall exhibition, such as a county fair. A smoke grenade will also be dropped on the peas by a competition director to indicate to an aircraft approaching jumprun that winds on the ground have become too hazardous for safe landings. Jumpers will also watch for smoke from "natural" situations such as chimneys and fires, to gauge wind direction during canopy control toward the DZ.

"To smoke it in" means to drop in free-fall below the generally accepted altitudes of 2,500 to 2,000 feet. *Smoking it in* during competition such as a Conference meet or a turkey meet may be cause for grounding.

Split saddle: Harness with separate leg straps.

Spot: The art of determining the opening point, to get parachutists back to the general area of the DZ. Inept spotters often receive a chilly reception, when the load of jumpers ends up "in the boondocks"—acres or miles away from the DZ, especially on a hot day. Spotters who jump square parachutes are also occasionally received badly because their parachutes can get them back to the DZ when round jumpers may be stuck off where the weeds are high and uncut. Spotters who take separate passes are stuck with their own spot, of course.

Stability: The art of achieving a poised position in free-fall, usually face-to-earth. A stable position is a necessary achievement for all free-fall formations.

Stabilizer Panel: Panels at the bottom of the sides of parachutes such as the ParaCommander and at the bottom edges of squares.

Stacked openings: In large formation jumps, openings may be stacked, i.e., in a 30-man jump, ten may open at 5,000 feet, ten more at 4,000 feet and the last ten at 3,000 feet, for safety.

Stalling: Pulling down steering lines or risers to alter the forward drive of the parachute.

Stand-up landing: A landing done skillfully, with the shock taken by the knees; as opposed to a P.L.F.

Star: Formation achieved by linked free-fall jumpers. Since later formations have involved diamonds, triangles, lines and other geometric symbols, the star is now sometimes called a *round*.

Static line: Unbreakable line which opens the parachutist's container automatically. Static lines are usually 15 feet long—long enough to clear the tail of the aircraft. Military paratroop jumps are almost always static line jumps; most novice jumpers learn on the static line and most of their gear is military surplus.

Steering lines: Lines which end in *toggles* on the jumper's risers. The parachute can be steered to the left or right by pulling down on the left or right toggle, which alters the flying configuration of the parachute. *Sawing* or rapid alternate pulling of the toggles usually does little good and only scares the novice when not much happens to the parachute.

Stick: Military slang. A partial or complete load of static-line paratroops dropped on the same DZ.

Stiffener: Metallic plate at the top of the ripcord housing and container to maintain a clear channel for the ripcord and housing and to prevent a pack closure by a stuck ripcord. Used on old-style containers. Containers that employ the throw-away pilot chute have no need for a stiffener because the ripcord (the bridle line for the pilot chute) is velcroed to the harness.

Stirrup: Elastic band holding the leg of the jumpsuit tight to the foot of the jumper.

Stowing band: Rubber band used to tuck away the suspension lines neatly and to aid in a neat, clean deployment of the lines during the opening sequence.

Streamer: Malfunction in which the sleeve elongates, or the bag clears the jumper, but the parachute does not emerge (or emerge fast enough). Usually means a cutaway.

Strut: Diagonal brace between the wing, of a Cessna or other similar aircraft, and the bottom of the fuselage. Novice jumpers are told to hold the strut until the Jumpmaster gives the command "Go!" All Jumpmasters have stories about novice jumpers who fail to let go of the strut on command and are either pushed or thrown off the step.

Student jumper: Person who has gone through the ground school but hasn't yet made his or her first jump.

Style: The art of acrobatics (front loop, back loop, barrel-roll) in free-fall done as quickly and as smoothly as possible in competition. Slowly falling out of favor; most jumpers with experience are working toward RW competition.

Style tuck: Compressed position roughly similar to a "Cannonball" position in diving, with the face down. The Style tuck allows the sky diver to complete the *style series* in minimum time.

Surplus: Army, Navy, or Air Force equipment used largely for novice jumping. What most of us learned with.

Suspension line: The lines connecting the *canopy* to the *harness*, at the *risers*, with *connector links*.

T.S.O.: Technical Standard Order. Government authorized gear. Equipment must be T.S.O.'ed for use in national competition.

T-10: A surplus main parachute. Originally non-steerable.

Target: Center disc used in competition. Generally 3 and 15/16th inches (ten centimeters) in diameter.

Temporary Locking Pins: Used during the packing of a reserve; must be removed before use.

Terminal: The ultimate and faster drop rate in free-fall. A trade-off between the pull of gravity and the drag of the jumper's gear and body position. Usually around 120 m.p.h. A reserve opening at terminal is an awesome experience because the reserve opens faster than a main (usually) and thus exposes the jumper to a harder opening shock. Most RW formations are attempted at terminal because of the momentum which the jumper can use to change positions, and move across the sky. Non-terminal RW offers the sky diver little leverage with which to work.

Three-Ring Circus: Three-ring capewell cutaway system sold with the Wonderhog.

Throw-away pilot chute: Pilot chute designed without coil spring. Made to be folded up like a pocket handkerchief and stowed in a pocket along the harness. In free-fall, to deploy the main, the jumper pulls the throw-away airstream; the pilot chute is attached to a *bridle cord*, which pulls the bag or pod out of the container. The advantages of the throw-away pilot chute are: without a coil spring it packs smaller and, since the sky diver throws the pilot chute to his side, it enters clear air beside him and thus offers little chance for a hesitation in the turbulent air over the jumper's back. New, state-of-the-art-design (introduced about 1976-1977).

Tie-down straps: Straps which connect the reserve with the jumper's harness to prevent the reserve from bouncing around in free-fall, which can be annoying, if not dangerous.

Toggles: Wooden pegs used to aid the jumper's hold on the steering lines.

Total: Pack closure. No parachute comes off the sky diver's back after a ripcord pull.

Track: Body position with the head and torso lower than the legs; allows the sky diver to pick up extensive distance. The sky diver makes his body into a wing and extends his "forward glide."

Tri-conical: Type of reserve canopy design.

Two-five: Common abbreviation for altitude (2,500 feet). Jumpers will abbreviate all altitudes, i.e., "I'm booked for a 7,5 (7,500 feet) jump, then a 12,5 (12,500 feet) jump in the Beech."

U.S.P.A.: United States Parachute Association, headquartered in Washington, D.C., the governing body for all sport jumping in the United States. Offers liability insurance, a monthly magazine *Parachutist* and other benefits to members.

Waiver: Legal release that most parachute clubs ask jumpers to sign relieving the club of responsibility in case of injury. Note: in many states, the waiver is of little good (to the club) except to warn the prospective parachutist that he may be engaging in a risky participatory sport. Some states do not allow anyone to sign away responsibility for injury or death.

Water jump: Deliberate jump into a body of water (lake or river) for a demo jump or for U.S.P.A. license purposes.

Wave-off: A safety measure, especially when other jumpers are in free-fall in the immediate area. Before pulling his ripcord, the sky diver waves his arms energetically horizontally across his chest to warn other sky divers that he will very soon pull his ripcord. A wave-off is done to avoid sky diver-canopy collisions.

Whuffo: Any spectator not acquainted with the pomp and glories of skydiving. So named after an apocryphal farmer who watched sky divers and then asked "wha' fo' you jump outta them airplanes, fo' "?

Wind: Sometimes a hazard to jumpers. U.S.P.A. recommends no sport jumping, at least for novices, in winds higher than 8 m.p.h.

Wind Drift Indicator: Length of brightly colored crepe paper (usually yellow) weighted to fall at a normal parachute rate tossed from the plane at opening height to judge wind currents in the air and thus make a determination of the *opening point* which will take the parachutists along a *wind line* to the *disc*. Note: The *exit point* and the *opening point* are seldom the same place in the sky.

Wind line: A direct line from the opening point to the target. Because of their forward drive capabilities, square parachutists are seldom worried about the wind line.

Wing: Square or ram-air parachute, called a wing because of its appearance and flying capabilities.

Wonderhog: One type of tandem system sold under that name.

Wrist mount: Velcro band used to attach an altimeter on the jumper's wrist where it is visible.

W.S.C.R.: Women's Star Crest Recipient.

W.S.C.S.: Women's Star Crest Soloist.

XX-rated: Jumper who has been in a 20-man formation.

Zapped out: A jumper who became unstable out the door (or) who broke up a formation.

*There are a thousand-and-one
questions about skydiving
which usually begin "But what if...?"*

Questions and Answers

Those who have only seen sport parachuting or skydiving on "The Wide World of Sports" or other similar programs often have a naive or misguided idea about what sport parachuting is like. Those who have only seen a demonstration jump at a county fair often have questions that they never really get answered correctly.

The following are questions which are usual "But what if . . ." questions that whuffo's commonly ask about the sport of parachuting and skydiving:

How many people across the country are sky divers?

The United States Parachute Association currently lists between 30,000 and 35,000 annual members throughout the country. Presumably, there are some active sky divers who do not belong to the national association. 35,000 seems a general figure.

How does skydiving compare with other sports in popularity?

Skydiving seems always destined to be a minor sport, because of the obvious dangers, because it appeals primarily to the young (college-aged participants) and because of other factors like suitable climate, availability of a local dropzone and so on. It is perhaps fortunate that skydiving *will* remain a minor sport—individuals select themselves *into* the sport primarily because they have always had a healthy curiosity about skydiving. These are the individuals who perform best, rather than those with a lukewarm interest in the sport.

What is the minimum age for sport parachuting?

Usually 18; sometimes, depending on local laws, 21. In some locals, an individual may begin at 16 with a notarized consent form signed by his or her parents. The nearest local sport parachute club is the best source of information regarding legal age to begin.

Do many older people get involved in jumping?

George McCulloch, featured elsewhere in this book, began when he was 55. He is now in his mid-70s and still active. Others have begun at the same age. The majority of active sky divers began when they were in college, however, and the majority of sky divers in the sport are roughly 18 to 35.

At what altitude do jumpers usually make their dives?

Beginners usually start at 2,500 feet to 2,900 feet. First free-fall jumps are usually made at 2,800 to 3,500 feet. As the jumper becomes more and more experienced, he jumps higher and higher until he is jumping regularly from 7,500 feet.

What kind of a free-fall—what length of time—is a jump from 7,500 feet?

The jumper ought to begin the opening sequence at, or slightly below 3,000 feet, so he or she is sitting under a good parachute at 2,500 feet. A free-fall from 7,500 feet to 2,500 feet usually takes 30 seconds and the sky diver is falling at approximately 120 miles per hour, depending on size, weight and body position.

How about higher jumps? What is free-fall time from 10,500 feet or 12,000 feet?

10,500 feet to 2,500 feet is a free-fall of about 45 seconds; 12,5 (as it is commonly abbreviated) to 2,5 is a free-fall of about 60 seconds.

What's the highest anyone has jumped from successfully?

Colonel Joe Kittinger's jump from 102,800 feet, featured elsewhere in this book, has the highest successful jump. He spent over four and one-half minutes in free-fall down to a canopy ride which began at 18,000 feet.

My boyfriend wants me to learn to jump because he is a jumper and loves it. I don't know . . . I'm scared of it . . . should a person jump to please someone else?

Jumping to please someone else is the worst motivation to begin the sport; self-motivation is the best reason to learn how to jump. The simplest answer is: No. Never learn how to skydive (or attempt any other active sport) just to please someone.

Is jumping as hazardous as it might appear? What is the fatality rate for jumping?

The rate of fatalities on a national level has remained relatively constant for the last ten or fifteen years, averaging between 25 and 45 deaths per year. While all sky divers mourn the loss of friends who have died during a sport jump, most jumpers believe that the fatality rate is well within safe limits (other licensing organizations such as the state, local officials and the Federal Aviation Administration, which takes an active part in parachute activities nationally, also concur). The 35,000 or so active sky divers make *about* three and one-half million sport jumps per year. Thus the fatality rate is roughly one in 100,000 jumps.

Is it more dangerous than other sports?

On a national level, with 25-45 fatalities per year, it is considerably less dangerous than many other sports and activities.

Is there a common mishap, like "tennis elbow"?

All jumpers must "come down" sometime, so the common feature of all jumps is ground contact. Thus most common are sprained ankles, twisted ankles and twisted wrists upon landing. But there is nothing specifically called "sky diver's ankle," like "tennis elbow."

Is skydiving much of a spectator sport or is it mainly a solitary pleasure?

Many jumpers bring their wives, boyfriends, or girlfriends out to the local dropzone on a regular basis and it is a beautiful sport from a spectator's view, but usually, it is a participants' sport, not a spectator sport.

Are there many famous people who enjoy the sport?

Johnny Carson, star of "The Tonight Show" on NBC TV made a classic free-fall from 12,500 feet some years ago. He has occasionally had sky divers on his program and has commented that he wished he could have the time for more jumping. Paul Williams, the composer-singer-actor has made a number of jumps. Sadly, however, skydiving is not a sport which attracts the famous and infamous, like golf or tennis.

What type of airplane do people usually jump from?

About 85 percent of all the sport jumping in this country is done from the various types of Cessna light aircraft. The Cessna 182 model is probably the most universally popular jump aircraft in the country, if not the world. Sky divers have been known to jump away from, and off the edge of, anything that can take them to jump height. Other popular jump aircraft are the Twin Beech and the DC-3.

Is there such a thing as a "professional sky diver" or is the sport mainly a hobby?

For almost all participants, it is a hobby. Very few have made the sport a profession. Many stuntmen and women in Hollywood are experienced parachutists, but "professional sky divers" are extremely rare.

Is it true that you need a license to skydive?

Those who only wish to satisfy their curiosity by making a few token jumps don't need a license. But serious parachutists begin working toward their licenses, plural. See the chapter on "Wings, Licenses, and Ratings," for an explanation of the licensing procedures.

Does skydiving have its own slang?

Yes, and it is highly colorful too. See the chapter on "Cheapos, PC's, downwinders and tracks" for an explanation of most of the common terms in parachuting and skydiving.

What's the average number of jumps most sky divers make in a month, or a year?

There is no average number of jumps among jumpers.

However, as a general guideline, anyone who makes 100 jumps or more each year must be considered a "hardcore" jumper.

What's the basic equipment necessary for skydiving?

The parachutist needs a main parachute, a reserve parachute, altimeter for free-fall jumping, helmet (motorcycle type or hockey helmet) and jumpsuit.

Is this equipment expensive?

A good "rag" chute—a "cheapo" used for a main—can cost $150 to $350 or more new. An intermediate-level main parachute such as a ParaCommander or PC-type (Starlite, Sierra, Sparrow or Russian PC) can cost $400 to $500 new, $200 and up used. A new square or wing may cost over $700 new; $300 and up used. A good reserve runs more than $100 used, $300 or so new. Helmets are $15 to $30 or more; jumpsuits vary from $45 to $100 for the best RW jumpsuit available. All in all, parachuting and snow skiing are roughly comparable in costs.

Are helmets mandatory?

Yes, although many experienced jumpers are now using lightweight hockey helmets rather than the older, heavier motorcycle helmets. Some experienced sky divers are using "frappe hats," lightweight leather skull caps. These are not recommended for novice jumpers.

Are jumpsuits padded?

No. Jumpsuits serve to help the sky diver stabilize in the air rather than the World War Two paratroop use for the jumpsuit as protection for the landing. Modern jumpsuits have "elephant bells" arms and legs to help the jumper in the same way that natural webbing helps the flying squirrel "fly."

Do jumpers need special boots—if so, made of what?

For many years, most jumpers used special "French jump boots," which were flexible but bulky and looked like ski boots. Now most experienced sky divers jump in jogging shoes, favoring the lightness and feel over the bulk of the older boots. Jump boots are still urged on novice jumpers until they get used to the ground contact.

How large are the actual parachutes?

A typical round parachute is about 26 feet in diameter. Reserves are 24 to 26 feet in diameter.

Do jumpers always wear reserve parachutes?

Yes. Always. Some parachutists wear "piggyback" rigs with the reserve on the top of the backpack. The reserve is not as noticeable as the old-style front reserve, but all jumpers carry two parachutes at all times.

How often are they necessary?

On the average, once in over one hundred jumps. This varies with the sky diver. Some inept sky divers need to use their reserves several times a year; others go without using a reserve for any reason for several years. It depends on the packing job of the main parachute, and on the expertise of the jumper. Needless to say, most jumpers pack their own parachutes *verrry carefullllyy*.

Okay. How long does it take to pack a main parachute?

Five to fifteen minutes, on the average.

What is the reaction of most beginning parachutists to their first jump?

They never forget it. Emotions range from curiosity, to ecstasy, to anxiety, to complete absorption in a world they scarcely dreamed existed.

Do parachutists usually land near a target or is the landing more haphazard?

Parachute centers usually provide a circle of pea gravel, sawdust, sand or plastic chips to land in, with a target disc in the center. Winds may, however, blow the parachutist away from the target. The parachutist eventually learns to control his parachute and judge winds so as not to land continually "out in the boondocks" . . .

When is one considered an "expert" skydiver?

When a jumper has a class "C" license, a "D" license, an SCR or an SCS, he or she is usually considered an expert; or if the jumper has the equivalent in jumps and experience for the "C" or "D" license. The chapter on "Wings, Licenses, and Ratings" lists qualifications for those earned licenses and awards.

What does it take to be a Jumpmaster and Instructor?

Again, the chapter on "Wings, Licenses and Ratings" has the qualification for these earned ratings.

Are there many private skydiving schools?

Yes, there are several hundred parachute centers throughout the country which offer first jump training and advanced free-fall techniques, equipment rental and jump aircraft. If there are no listings in your telephone book, write for the "Drop Zone Directory" from the United States Parachute Association, Washington, D.C. The complete address is listed in the Bibliography.

How long is the beginning—"first jump course"?

Usually two to four hours. In many cases, the student begins the course early on a Saturday morning, for instance, finishes the course and has a small lunch and then makes the first jump later in the day, if weather conditions permit. Instructors don't usually allow the student to "come back next week" for the first jump because the student is likely to forget various aspects of the course of instruction and have to be re-briefed. The sport parachute first jump course, however, doesn't take weeks and weeks, like paratroop training does.

What is the cost for the first jump course?

From "bargain basement" rates like $35 for major parachute centers which specialize in first jump students, to $75 and more for smaller operations. The average seems to be about $55 nationally, which covers the ground class, all equipment needed for the first jump and the plane ride to jump altitude. Generally speaking, however, if the student chooses not to make the first jump, no refund is made.

How much are second and subsequent jumps?

As the student gains in experience, the cost per jump goes down. The second jump might, for instance, cost $35; the third $17, the fourth jump $15; the fifth $12.50 or so. After the student is in free-fall, he or she pays for the equipment on a jump-by-jump basis and also pays for the "taxi ride" to jump altitude, also on a jump-by-jump basis, usually on the ticket system.

How much do expert sky divers pay for their plane rides?

The usual rule of thumb is $1 for every thousand feet: 4,500 feet, $4.50; 7,500 feet would be $7.50. Above that, the jumper pays slightly less than $1 per thousand feet: a jump from 10,500 feet might be $8.00; a jump from 12,500 might be $10.

How much are pilots paid?

The parachute center usually works some sort of "trade-off" with the pilot: he gets his airtime free for working flying the jump-plane, or he flys all day Saturday and jumps all day Sunday free. Most parachute centers operate on limited budgets and trade facilities for work.

Do Jumpmasters and Instructors get paid?

They usually get all their jumping free, in exchange for their work.

How many people usually jump together at one time?

The usual group is four at a time, eight or ten at one time; above ten calls for a large aircraft or two or more aircraft and most certainly experienced sky divers. The largest free-fall formation is approaching 60 sky divers in a round star (60 may be surpassed by the time this book is published).

Is skydiving becoming more or less popular?

It appears to be becoming slightly more popular year by year with the increase coming from college-aged learners.

Do many military paratroopers take up the sport as a hobby after leaving the service?

Rarely; military jumping is rough and hazardous and paratroops are quite happy to leave jumping, thank you. It is too much of a "busman's holiday" for many of them to return, even though sport parachuting is easier, the gear lighter, and the landing much softer.

How is the sport regulated—is there an "association" like golf?

The sport is governed by the United States Parachute Association, very much like the P.G.A.; for governing purposes, the country is subdivided into twelve Conferences, each with an elected Conference Director.

How is the government involved?

The government, in the form of the Federal Aviation Administration (F.A.A.) establishes rules and laws concerning safe sport parachuting; state and local laws also govern the sport. Licensing of sport parachutists, however, is done by the U.S. Parachute Association.

Are there many magazines available on the sport?

There are two magazines: *Parachutist* and *Spotter*. There is also a tabloid newspaper, *Skydiving*, published every three weeks. They are listed in the Bibliography.

Are there many women sky divers?

The average is ten men for every one woman. There is no reason, however, why many more women shouldn't enter the sport. Women are more agile, lighter and land softer than men. Some parachute centers encourage a "locker-room comaraderie," however, which turns some women off regarding the sport. Many women don't like the "jock image" which some male sky divers encourage.

The expression "hitting the silk" is still heard regarding parachuting. Are parachutes made of silk?

They were—until about the time of World War Two, when nylon was invented. Now all parachutes are made from "ripstop" (untearable) nylon, the same fabric sailboat sails are made of.

How long will a nylon parachute last?

Indefinitely, with care. The author has a 1964-manufacture parachute that has probably 1,000 jumps on it and looks brand new.

What happens if the main parachute fails?

The chapter on the first jump experience explains how a parachutist "cuts away" his main and comes down on his reserve.

What happens if both main and reserve fail?

Statistically, this is so removed as to be a meaningless possibility. If you are bothered about that possibility, you better really be worried about a car crash on the way to and from the airport: that kind of accident is a much more real possibility.

Is there much of an impact upon landing?

Less than jumping off the roof of your car. Actually, parachutists learn the PLF (parachute landing fall) which is much like the sideways fall of a snow skier. The landing is usually comparable to jumping off your kitchen table.

Is there much literature available about jumping?

There are several books about jumping technique and some about general aspects of jumping. The Bibliography lists all currently available books.

Can handicapped people jump?

Yes, Jerry Irwin, one of the nation's best free-fall photographers, lost an eye in a ground accident unrelated to skydiving. Al Krueger, captain of one of the nationally known skydiving teams, "Captain Hook and the Sky Pirates" (discussed elsewhere in this book) has an artificial arm. Neither consider themselves handicapped in the least and jump much better than most of their contemporaries.

Where do sky divers get their equipment—are there special stores or do they buy it at skydiving schools?

Both. ParaGear Equipment Company, outside of Chicago; McElfish, in Dallas; SSE, Incorporated in New Jersey and Pioneer Parachutes, in Manchester, Connecticut, are four of the biggest dealers. Many skydiving centers sell gear and there is usually a big swapping business among jumpers. All major manufacturers and mail-order dealers advertise regularly in the parachute magazines.

Can sky divers hear each other during a free-fall jump—if they are holding each other's hands?

No. Free-fall jumpers are falling at 120 miles-per-hour and must communicate with signals, nods of the head or waves of the arms. Sky divers can yell at each other while they are holding hands and yet not be heard. Under the canopy, however, sky divers can yell at each other and be heard, within reason.

You have used the terms parachuting and skydiving. Are they interchangeable?

The word *parachuting* usually means the art of canopy control—steering—during the descent. *Skydiving* refers to the free-fall, before the canopy is deployed. All successful *skydives* eventually involve *parachuting;* not all parachute jumps (i.e., military paratroop jumps and sport static line jumps) involve skydiving.

Can you breathe during free-fall?

Yes. Breathing is as natural as it is on the ground.

Isn't everything a blur at those speeds?

No. Most sky divers report a heightened sense of sight, even without goggles which are usually worn.

Do sky divers use colorful language during the plane ride?

Oh, yes. If they miss the right exit point, the experienced sky diver may resort to the use of our basic four-letter words, such as "rats" or "gosh!" If the pilot is forced because of clouds or air traffic to spend an extra half-hour in the air on one load, he may resort to "darn!"

Do sky divers ever yell "Geronimo" during the jump?

Only in John Wayne movies.

Licenses, Wings, and Ratings
These are your . . .

Personal Achievements

Many sky divers love the sport because there is always a goal to work toward, a new achievement, a new conquest, a new physical and mental (and perhaps psychological) standard to achieve. Novice jumpers often continue in the sport "Until I get my 'A' Class license" or "Until I get my SCR" or "D license." They also work toward some other objective—there is a better goal up the road, demanding more jumps, more expertise, better gear, bigger aircraft.

Because there are so many goals and achievements to pursue, many jumpers, upon reaching their "Gold Wings" —1,000 jumps—declare flatly they are trying for 2,000 jumps, or 3,000. (Much to the dismay of the spouse who had hoped that 1,000 jumps would be enough.)

The following are the Licenses, Wings, and Ratings in the order of general difficulty. Requirements, achievements and organizations to contact to apply for the award are all listed.

U. S. Parachute Association Awards

Novice: "Class A License"

Requirements: Must have completed 25 free-fall jumps, including:
- 12 controlled delays of at least 10 seconds
- 6 controlled delays of at least 20 seconds
- 3 controlled delays of at least 30 seconds
- 10 free-fall jumps landing within 50 meters of target during which the novice selected the exit and opening points
- Demonstrated ability to hold a heading during free-fall and make 360-degree turns to both the right and the left
- Demonstrated ability to Jumpmaster himself or herself, to include independent selection of the proper altitude and proper use of correct exit and opening points
- Demonstrated ability to pack his own main parachute properly and conduct safety checks on his or her parachute and other parachutist's equipment prior to a jump
- Obtained a logbook endorsement by a USPA Instructor/Examiner, Club Safety Officer (CSO) or Area Safety Officer (ASO) that the jumper has had training for unintentional water landings
- Passed a written examination conducted by a USPA Instructor/Examiner, USPA Instructor, his CSO or ASO.

License Fee: $5.00

Qualifications: Persons who hold a Class A license are certified to jumpmaster themselves, to perform water jumps, pack their own main parachute and compete in USPA competitions (other than Conference and National Championships).

Apply to: Licensing Department, United States Parachute Association, 806 Fifteenth St., N.W. Suite 444, Washington, D.C. 20005.

Intermediate: "Class B License"

Requirements: Must meet all requirements for the "A" license, including making 50 controlled free-fall parachute jumps, including fifteen delays of at least 30 seconds and two delays of at least 45 seconds.
- Demonstrated ability to complete two alternate 360-degree flat turns to the right and left (figure 8) followed by a backloop in free-fall in ten seconds or less
- Landed with 25 meters of target center on 10 jumps during which the parachutist selected the exit and opening points

- Demonstrated ability to control and vary rate of descent and lateral movement in free-fall
- Demonstrated ability to engage in relative work safely involving at least two jumpers. This includes:
    1) demonstrated ability to perform door exits
    2) demonstrated ability to move away from jumpers horizontally in free-fall and check the sky around him so that he may deploy his parachute without danger or collision with a fellow parachutist
- Demonstrated ability to keep track of other canopies in the air and remain a safe distance from them
- Passed a written examination conducted by a USPA Instructor/Examiner, USPA Instructor, CSO or ASO

License Fee: $10.00

Qualifications: B license holders are qualified to jumpmaster themselves, pack their own main parachute, are eligible for selection as Club Safety Officer, are recognized as qualified to perform night and water jumps, to perform relative work and to participate in USPA competitions (other than Conference and National Championships). They may also participate in record attempts.

Apply to: USPA, Washington, D.C.

Advanced: "Class C License"

Requirements: Must meet all requirements for the "B" license and additionally must make 100 controlled parachute jumps including thirty controlled delays of at least 30 seconds and five controlled delays of at least 45 seconds.

- Demonstrated ability to perform a controlled international series (figure 8, backloop, figure 8, backloop) in free-fall in 18 seconds or less
- Landed within 15 meters of target center on 25 free-fall jumps during which the parachutist independently selected the exit and opening points
- Demonstrated ability to "track"
- Demonstrated ability to control and coordinate descent and horizontal movement by exiting the aircraft after at least two other experienced jumpers and successfully entering a formation third or later on the same jump
- Passed a written test conducted by a USPA Instructor/Examiner, CSO, or ASO.

License Fee: $15.00

Qualifications: C license holders are certified to jumpmaster licensed parachutists, pack their own main parachute, are eligible for election as Club Safety Officer and Area Safety Officer, may enter USPA competitions (including Conference competitions), may make relative work jumps, night, water and exhibition jumps, may participate in record attempts and are eligible for the USPA Jumpmaster and Instructor ratings.

Apply to: USPA, Washington, D.C.

Expert: "Class D License"

Requirements: Must meet all requirements for the C license. Additionally, must have made 200 controlled parachute jumps, including:
- 100 delays of at least 20 seconds
- 50 delays of at least 30 seconds
- 10 delays of at least 45 seconds
- 5 delays of at least 60 seconds
- Demonstrated ability to perform the following maneuvers on heading in 18 seconds or less (in sequence): Backloop, frontloop, left turn, right turn, right barrel roll, left barrel roll; or successfully entered a star sixth or later, which must be held stable for an additional five seconds or 1,000 feet
- Landed within two meters of target center on 10 freefall delays during which the parachutist independently selected the exit and opening points
- Made one night parachute jump with a delay of at least 20 seconds, with certification of prior night jump training by a USPA Instructor/Examiner, USPA Instructor, CSO or ASO. Jump must be approved by the ASO in accordance with accepted basic safety rules
- Passed a written test given by a USPA Inspector/Examiner, USPA Instructor, or his ASO.

License fee: $20.00

Qualifications: The D license holder is qualified to jumpmaster licensed parachutists, pack his or her main parachute, participate in all competitions at the local, Conference and National level, participate in record attempts, make relative work jumps, night and water and exhibition jumps. The D license holder is eligible for election or appointment as

Jumpmaster, Instructor, Instructor/Examiner, eligible for appointment as Area Safety Officer or Club Safety Officer.
Apply to: USPA, Washington, D.C.

Note: USPA A, B, C, and D licenses are automatically renewed annually when the parachutist renews his USPA membership. All licenses require keeping a logbook of jumps.

Relative Work Achievements

Recognition for achievement in free-fall relative work accomplishments is governed by a private, independent organization, the Bob Buquor Memorial Star Crest Association. Bob Buquor, a California relative worker during the early days of RW, was drowned in 1965 off Malibu Beach, California, during the making of a free-fall film. There are four main achievements honored by the Star Crest Association.

Star Crest Recipient (SCR): Must have participated in a free-fall formation involving eight or more sky divers held together for a minimum of five seconds. SCR qualified to enter the formation from first to seventh place. The SCR is *the* internationally-known achievement for free-fall expertise.
Application fee: $10.00
Apply to: Bob Buquor Memorial Star Crest, P. O. Box 4277, Bakersfield, California 93307

SCS: (Star Crest Soloist Award) is given to those who qualify by entering a formation eighth or later (on large-star formation). The formation must be held stable for five seconds or longer.
Application fee: $10.00
Apply to: Memorial Star Crest Association, Bakersfield

Night SCR: The Night SCR is awarded to sky divers who enter an eight-man (or larger) formation, held for five seconds, after the full dark of night has fallen (one hour after sunset to one hour before dawn)
Application fee: $10.00
Apply to: Memorial Star Crest Association, Bakersfield

SCSA: (Star Crest Sky Diver Award) is achieved by eight or more jumpers passing through a hoop held by two jumpers and forming an eight-man (or larger) formation on the other side of the hoop. The first of the two hoop flyers to exit the aircraft must remain on the jumper's left side as they pass through the hoop. The hoop must have a maximum I. D. of 36 inches. A minimum of ten sky divers are required to earn the award and the two hoop flyers are included.
Application fee: $10.00
Apply to: Memorial Star Crest Association, Bakersfield

Note: No Starcrest awards are valid if any of the participants are holding onto or hooked to another jumper upon exiting the aircraft. The Starcrest Association also makes awards to participants in 16-man formations, 24-man formations and military 10-man formations (and also has information about Women's SCR awards). Write the association for additional details about these awards.

Canopy Relative Work Achievements

The newest form of achievement awards for skydiving is the "CRW" Canopy Relative Work qualifications. CRW is the art of "flying" two or more canopies which are interconnected; i.e., one jumper holding onto the top of a lower canopy with his feet. The formation is often a "stack" (vertical formation) but may be a diamond or other geometric pattern. All CRW applicants must hold the formation together and interconnected completely for 60 seconds.

Four Stack Emblem: Must be a member of a four-canopy formation, as indicated above, for 60 seconds. Jacket patch awarded.
Application fee: $3.50
Apply to: USPA, Washington, D.C.

C.C.R. (Canopy Crest Recipient): Must have been a member of an eight-canopy formation, held for 60 seconds.
Application fee: $5.00
Apply to: USPA, Washington, D.C.

C.C.S. (Canopy Crest Soloist): Must have entered the formation eighth or later and held for 60 seconds
Application fee: $5.00
Apply to: USPA, Washington, D.C.

USPA Ratings

The USPA certified Jumpmaster is qualified to review novice training, supervise novices in the aircraft and supervise novice jumpers on static line and beginning free-fall jumps.

An applicant for the Jumpmaster rating must have successfully completed a Jumpmaster Certification Course. Prior to taking and passing the course, the candidate must show expertise in the following areas:

- Received personal instruction in handling static line equipment and aircraft procedures, by a USPA Instructor or Instructor/Examiner. Must include aircraft emergencies, emergency landings and other types of aircraft emergencies
- Demonstrated competence by jumpmastering ten free-fall novices, while being supervised by an Instructor or I/E
- Demonstrated competence in jumpmastering static line jumpers, in which a parachutist holding an A license or higher acts as a novice during the jump (by BSR's, no Jumpmaster candidate may jumpmaster an actual novice until he or she earns the Jumpmaster rating)
- Demonstrated a knowledge of three of the four common types of static line rigging procedures (breakcord; cone, pins and ring; pins and elastic cords; and direct bag)
- Demonstrated knowledge of one type of automatic opening device
- Assisted in teaching at least two first jump courses
- Assisted in teaching novices on at least three dummy ripcord pulls, including ground training, the jump, and post-jump critique
- Assisted in teaching two first free-fall novices, including pre-jump, jump and after-jump critiques
- Received training from an Instructor or I/E on such common problems as poor exit, poor arch, loss of stability, et cetera

- Demonstrated knowledge to teach spotting
- Demonstrated knowledge to teach pre-jump briefings
- Demonstrated knowledge to teach free-fall techniques such as flat turns, free-fall maneuvers, back loops and tracking
- Must hold a current C or D license
- Passed the USPA Jumpmaster Certification Course.

Application fee: $10.00 payable at Jumpmaster Certification Course beginning.

Apply to: USPA, Washington, or nearest Conference Director.

The USPA certified **Instructor** is qualified to teach the basic first jump course and also instruct novice free-fall students in the art of parachuting and skydiving.

The United States Parachute Association writes that the Instructor shall possess the USPA Jumpmaster rating and have successfully completed the Instructor Certification Course. In addition, the Instructor must have:

- Jumpmastered at least 25 static line novice jumps
- Jumpmastered at least 15 free-fall novice jumpers
- Assisted in teaching at least four complete First Jump Courses
- Demonstrated competence to teach a First Jump Course by teaching one course under the supervision of a USPA Instructor or Instructor/Examiner
- Personally taught at least three novices on the first free-fall jumps
- Assisted in teaching at least two persons to pack a main parachute
- Participated in at least ten successful three-person stars (or larger)
- Prepared complete lesson plans for novice instructor, beginning at the first jump course and covering all topics of instruction through completion of the A license
- Taught at least one parachutist to jump an advanced canopy (ParaCommander or PC type) including one jump in which the parachutist lands within 25 meters of target center
- Demonstrated ability to teach relative work techniques successfully
- Demonstrated ability to teach night and water jump

techniques and successfully completed class C and D requirements for water and night jumps.

Applicants must pass the Instructor Certification Course.

Application fee: $10.00 payable at the beginning of Instructor Certification Course.

Apply to: USPA, Washington, or nearest Conference Director.

The USPA **Instructor/Examiner** rating is the highest earned rating in national parachuting. The I/E rating is the hardest to obtain and the national headquarters requires service, ability and generally high levels of competence for this rating.

According to USPA regulations, the I/E must "be able to instruct in all areas of parachuting. He must be able to answer any questions that may be asked by parachutists desiring to make high altitude jumps or record attempts; he must be able to instruct in basic first aid that might be needed on the drop zone; and he must be able to teach packing and maintenance of parachutes and parachute equipment."

"In the public relations field the Instructor/Examiner should be capable of briefing local news media and the general public regarding the history and the future of parachuting. He will also serve local aviation circles in the capacity of a recognized expert in the area of all phases of parachuting."

To qualify for the I/E rating, the applicant must complete five areas of expertise:

1) Forward to the USPA national headquarters an application form and a fee of $30.

2) Take a written exam.

3) Qualify as a Federal Aviation Administration (FAA) Senior or Master rigger, and be rated to pack back and chest parachutes.

4) Complete a series of practical exams.

5) Be a USPA Instructor for at least one year and submit a list of character references.

The practical exam is the toughest part of qualifying for the I/E rating. USPA demands that the applicant:

• Be capable of packing all types of back and chest-type parachutes

- Be capable of making all repairs that a rigger is authorized to perform
- Have at least two hours of total accumulated time in free-fall
  - Participate in at least 25 three-man stars (or larger)
  - Participate in one eight-man star (or larger)
  - Jumpmaster 100 static line novices
  - Jumpmaster at least 50 free-fall novices
  - Teach 15 complete First Jump Courses
  - Land within one meter of the target on 30 jumps
  - Assist in at least one Jumpmaster Certification Course
  - Assist in at least one Instructor Certification Course
  - Assist in organizing and conducting a night jump
  - Assist in organizing and conducting an intentional water jump
  - Take at least one photograph of another sky diver in free-fall
  - Enter at least one Conference meet and participate in any three of the following categories: style, competition, accuracy competition, 4-man RW or 10-man RW
  - Complete at least 500 free-fall parachute jumps
  - Participate in at least two demonstration jumps.

The USPA also recommends but does not require, that the applicant have attended a Physiological Flight Training Course and hold a current Red Cross Standard First Aid Card.

Application fee: $30.00

Apply to: USPA National Headquarters

Additionally, the USPA awards national recognition to sky divers with accumulated time as a sky diver. These awards include:

Gold Wings: awarded for 1,000 certified free-fall jumps

Apply to: USPA National Headquarters, Washington, D. C.

12-Hour Free-fall Award: for 12 hours or more accumulated time in free-fall

Apply to: USPA National Headquarters, Washington, D. C.

24-Hour Free-fall Award: for 24 hours or more accumulated time in free-fall

Apply to: USPA National Headquarters, Washington, D. C.

Diamond Wings: for 2,000 certified jumps
Apply to: USPA National Headquarters, Washington, D. C.

Double Diamond Wings: You'll never get there! (3,000 certified jumps)
Apply to: USPA National Headquarters, Washington, D. C.

Poetry and Fiction

FALLING

by James Dickey

> A 29-year-old stewardess fell . . . to her death tonight when she was swept through an emergency door that suddenly sprang open . . . The body . . . was found . . . three hours after the accident.– *The Times.*

The states when they black out and lie there rolling   when they turn   To something transcontinental   move by drawing moonlight out of the great   One-sided stone hung off the starboard wing tip.   Some sleeper next to   An engine is groaning for coffee   and there is faintly coming in   Somewhere the vast beast-whistle of space. In the galley with its racks   Of trays   she rummages for a blanket   and moves in her slim tailored   Uniform to pin it over the cry at the top of the door.   As though she blew

The door down with a silent blast from her lungs   frozen she is black   Out finding herself   with the plane nowhere and her body taking by the throat   The undying cry of the void   falling   living   beginning to be something   That no one has ever been and lived through   screaming without enough air   Still neat   lipsticked   stockinged   girdled by

regulation   her hat   Still on   her arms and legs in no
world   and yet spaced also strangely   With utter placid
rightness on thin air   taking her time   she holds it   In
many places   and now, still thousands of feet from her
death   she seems   To slow   she develops interest   she
turns in her maneuverable body
To watch it. She is hung high up in the overwhelming middle
of things   in   her   Self   in low body-whistling wrapped
intensely   in all her dark dance-weight   Coming down from a
marvellous leap   with the delaying, dumbfounding ease   Of
a dream of being drawn   like endless moonlight to the harvest
soil   Of a central state of one's country   with a great
gradual warmth coming   Over her   floating   finding more
and more breath in what she has been using   For breath   as
the levels become more human   seeing clouds placed honestly
Below her left and right   riding slowly toward them   she
clasps it all   To her and can hang her hands and feet in it
in peculiar ways   and,   Her eyes opened wide by wind, can
open her mouth as wide   wider   and suck   All the heat
from the cornfields   can go down on her back with a feeling   Of stupendous pillows stacked under her   and can
turn   turn as to someone   In bed   smile, understood in
darkness   can go away   slant   slide   Off tumbling   into
the emblem of a bird with its wings half-spread   Or whirl
madly on herself   in endless gymnastics in the growing
warmth   Of wheatfields rising toward the harvest moon.
There is time to live   In superhuman health   seeing mortal
unreachable lights far down   seeing   An ultimate highway
with one late priceless car probing it   arriving   In a square
town   and off her starboard arm the glitter of water catches
The moon by its one shaken side   scaled, roaming silver   My
God it is good   And evil   lying in one after another of all
the positions for love   Making   dancing   sleeping   and
now cloud wisps at her   no   Raincoat   no matter   all
small towns brokenly brighter from inside   Cloud   she
walks over them like rain   bursts out to behold a Grey-
hound   Bus shooting light through its sides   it is the
signal to go straight   Down like a glorious diver   then feet
first   her skirt stripped beautifully   Up   her face in fear-
scented cloths   her legs   deliriously bare   then   Arms
out   she slow-rolls over   steadies out   waits for something

great To take control of her   trembles near feathers   planes head-down   The quick movements of bird-necks turning her head   gold eyes   the insight-eyesight of owls blazing into the hencoops   a taste for chicken overwhelming   Her   the long-range vision of hawks enlarging all human lights   of cars   Freight trains   looped bridges   enlarging the moon racing slowly   Through all the curves of a river   all the darks of the Midwest blazing   From within. A rabbit in a bush turns white   the smothering chickens   Huddle   for over them there is still time for something to live   With the streaming half-idea of a long stoop   a hurtling   a fall   That is controlled   that plummets as it wills   turns gravity   Into a new condition, showing its other side like a moon   shining New Powers   there is still time to live on a breath made of nothing   But the whole night   time for her to remember to arrange her skirt   Like a diagram of a bat   tightly it guides her   she has this flying-skin   Made of garments   and there are also those sky-divers on TV   sailing   In sunlight   smiling under their goggles   swapping batons back and forth   And He who jumped without a chute and was handed one by a diving   Buddy. She looks for her grinning companion   white teeth   nowhere   She is screaming   singing hymns   her thin human wings spread out   From her neat shoulders   the air beast-crooning to her   warbling   And she can no longer behold the huge partial form of the world   now   She is watching her country lose its evoked master shape   watching it lose   And gain   get back its houses and peoples   watching it bring up   Its local lights   single homes   lamps on barn roofs   if she fell   Into water she might live   like a diver   cleaving   perfect   plunge

Into another   heavy silver   unbreathable   slowing   saving Element: there is water   there is time to perfect all the fine   Points of diving   feet together   toes pointed   hands shaped right   To insert her into water like a needle   to come out healthily dripping   And be handed a Coca-Cola   there they are   there are the waters   Of life   the moon packed and coiled in a reservoir   *so let me begin   To plane across the night air of Kansas   opening my eyes superhumanly Bright to the damned moon   opening the natural wings of my jacket   By Don Loper   moving like a hunting owl*

toward the glitter of water   One cannot just fall   just tumble screaming all that time   one must use   It   she is now through with all   through all   clouds   damp   hair Straightened   the last wisp of fog pulled apart on her face like wool   revealing   New darks   new progressions of headlights along dirt roads   from chaos
And night   a gradual warming   a new-made, inevitable world of one's own   Country   a great stone of light in its waiting waters   hold   hold out   For water: who knows when what correct young woman must take up her body And fly   and head for the moon-crazed inner eye of Midwest imprisoned   Water   stored up for her for years   the arms of her jacket slipping   Air up her sleeves to go   all over her? What final things can be said   Of one who starts out sheerly in her body in the high middle of night   Air   to track down water like a rabbit where it lies like life itself   Off to the right in Kansas? She goes toward   the blazing-bare lake   Her skirts neat   her hands and face warmed more and more by the air   Rising from pastures of beans   and under her   under chenille bedspreads   The farm girls are feeling the goddess in them struggle and rise   brooding   On the scratch-shining posts of the bed   dreaming of female signs   Of the moon   male blood like iron   of what is really said by the moan   Of airlines passing over them at dead of Midwest midnight   passing   Over brush fires burning out in silence on little hills   and will wake   To see the woman they should be   struggling on the roof-tree to become   Stars. For her the ground is closer   water is nearer   she passes   It   then banks   turns   her sleeves fluttering differently as she rolls Out to face the east, where the sun shall come up from wheatfields   she must   Do something with water   fly to it   fall in it   drink it   rise   From it   but there is none left upon earth   the clouds have drunk it back   The plants have sucked it down   there are standing toward her only   The common fields of death   she comes back from flying to falling   Returns to a powerful cry   the silent scream with which she blew down   The coupled door of the airliner   nearly   nearly losing hold   Of what she has done   remembers   remembers the shape at the heart   Of cloud   fashionably swirling   remembers she still has time to die   Beyond explanation. Let her now take off her hat in

summer air the contour   Of cornfields   and have enough
time to kick off her one remaining   Shoe with the toes of
the other foot   to unhook her stockings   With calm fingers,
noting how fatally easy it is to undress in midair   Near death
when the body will assume without effort any position   Except the one that will sustain it   enable it to rise   live Not
die   nine farms hover close   widen   eight of them separate,
leaving   One in the middle   then the fields of that farm do
the same   there is no   Way to back off   from her chosen
ground   but she sheds the jacket   With its silver sad impotent wings   sheds the bat's guiding tailpiece   Of her
skirt   the lightning-charged clinging of her blouse   the intimate   Inner flying-garment of her slip in which she rides like
the holy ghost   Of a virgin   sheds the long wind-socks of
her stockings   absurd   Brassiere   then feels the girdle
required by regulations squirming   Off her: no longer monobuttocked   she feels the girdle flutter   shake   In her hand
and float   upward   her clothes rising off her   ascending
Into cloud   and fights away from her head the last sharp
dangerous shoe   Like a dumb bird   and now will drop
in   SOON   now will drop

In like this   the greatest thing that ever came to Kansas
down from all   Heights   all levels of American breath layered in the lungs   from the frail   Chill of space to the loam
where extinction slumbers in corn tassels   thickly   And
breathes like rich farmers counting   will come among them
after   Her last superhuman act   the last slow careful passing of her hands All over her unharmed body   desired by
every sleeper in his dream: Boys finding for the first time
their loins filled with heart's blood   Widowed farmers whose
hands float under light covers to find themselves   Arisen at
sunrise   the splendid position of blood unearthly drawn
Toward clouds   all feel something   pass over them as she
passes   Her palms over *her* long legs   *her* small breasts and
deeply between   Her thighs   her hair shot loose from all
pins   streaming in the wind   Of her body   let her come
openly   trying at the last second to land   On her back   This
is it   THIS

All those who find her impressed
In the soft loam   gone down   driven well into the image of

her body   The furrows for miles flowing in upon her where
she lies very deep   In her mortal outline   in the earth as it
is in cloud   can tell nothing   But that she is there   inexplicable   unquestionable   and remember   That something
broke in them as well   and began to live and die more   When
they walked for no reason into their fields to where the
whole earth   Caught her   interrupted her maiden flight
told her how to lie   she cannot   Turn   go away   cannot
move   cannot slide off it and assume another   Position no
sky-diver with any grin could save her   hold her in his
arms   Plummet with her   unfold above her his wedding
silks   she can no longer   Mark the rain with whirling
women that take the place of a dead wife   Or the goddess
in Norwegian farm girls   or all the backbreaking whores
of Wichita. All the known air above her is not giving up
quite one   Breath   it is all gone   and yet not dead   not
anywhere else   Quite   lying still in the field on her back
sensing the smells   Of incessant growth try to lift her   a
little sight left in the corner   Of one eye   fading   seeing
something wave   lies believing   That she could have made
it   at the best part of her brief goddess   State   to water
gone in head first   come out smiling   invulnerable   Girl in
a bathing-suit ad   but she is lying like a sunbather at the
last   Of moonlight   half-buried in her impact on the earth
not far   From a railroad trestle   a water tank   she could
see if she could   Raise her head from her modest hole   with
her clothes beginning   To come down all over Kansas   into
bushes   on the dewy sixth green   Of a golf course   one
shoe   her girdle coming down fantastically   On a clothesline, where it belongs   her blouse on a lightning rod:

Lies in the fields   in *this* field   on her broken back   as
though on   A cloud she cannot drop through   while farmers
sleepwalk without   Their women from houses   a walk like
falling toward the far waters   Of life   in moonlight   toward
the dreamed eternal meaning of their farms   Toward the
flowering of the harvest in their hands   that tragic cost

Feels herself go   go toward   go outward   breathes at
last fully   Not   and tries   less   once   tries   tries
   AH, GOD—

FIRST FLIGHT

by Steven Osterlund

>   Out of his delirious speech I pluck
>   Blind faith . . .
>   Vertigo triples; below us doll horses
>   scum and channel markers, the zigzag hem
>   of America
>   Industry's mephitic eruptions joggle
>   the Cessna at
>   five hundred feet, at a thousand we're
>   anchorites, mystics: greetings, God, is this
>   the fourth dimension?
>   I point to rectangles, my
> acrophobia's cured; ascent, perspective, abundant
>   power aloft
>   with the intelligent pilot
>   Oh higher, higher friend, smack into the sun
>   SMEAR me across it!

DIVERS

by Charles Ghigna

We were different when we returned to earth.
Too alone in our fall to forget,
we lost all trust in the touch of gentle hands.
The dropped baby in us grew.

We listened too long to a thinner wind,
climbed too close to a hollow sun,
stood one by one in the cockpit's open door,
left our mothered souls in the fading steel
of a Cessna's shaking belly,
stepped into a hand-less world,
stretched the corners of our eyes until they split,
watched an anvil earth fly up at us,
took our own umbilical cord in hand and ripped,
and fell like frightened spiders
who spin our frantic silk that clings to only air.

Fisheye shot of star building to completion. (Ray Cottingham photo)

THE SKYDIVER

by jeannie McCombs

Between the security of childhood and the insecurity
 of second childhood we find the SKYDIVER.
Skydivers are found everywhere, in bars, under bars,
behind bars, looking through bars, in trouble, in debt,
            in the air and in love.

Skydivers come in assorted sizes, shapes, and weights
in states of sobriety, misery and confusion.
Girls love them, mothers worry about them,
Unemployment Cheques support them,
and by some coincidence they manage to get along

with each other. The Skydiver is laziness with a deck
of cards, a millionaire without a cent, bravery with a smile

The Skydiver is composite, sly as a fox, has the brains of an
idiot, the energy of a turtle, the sincerity of a liar, the
appetite of an elephant, the aspirations of a casanova,
the story of a hero. When he wants something it is usually
free jumps, more money, a good piece of tail. He dislikes
ASO's, getting up early, small planes, hot shot pilots (that
never hit the DZ), the week before his pay day, his girl's
father's curfew, and legs (that is a land lover). He likes
girls, women, females and all members of the opposite sex

No one can think of you so often and write so seldom
No one can get so much fun out of your letters, old jump
              suits and sex movies

The Skydiver is a magical creature, you can lock
him out of your house, but not out of your heart.
You can take him off your mailing list but not out of
              your mind.

THE PHANTOM TENTH MAN

by Jim Rogers

Flying Fred had cratered in
A week ago, and now and then
We saw the spot where he'd been killed
The hole in the ground had just been filled.

It made us stop and it made us think
But we shrugged our shoulders and drank our drinks;
We knew the score when he got his:
Jumping from planes is a dangerous biz.

Fred had given up students and he'd given up style
And he only saw the target every once in a while.

Most of the time he walked country roads
Having just come down from an eight-man load.

Time and again we'd heard Fred say,
"Now save a place, 'cause on the day
That this state sees a ten-man fly
I'm closing tenth before I die."

Well, thinking of what we'd heard Fred say
We decided to hold a memorial day.
The first ten-man still gleamed in our eyes
So on this day we'd give it a try.

With chewing gum and refrigerator tape
We put our Beech into real good shape.
The pilot grinned at the dripping oil
Then strapped on a rig and said, "Let's roll."

The Federal Man thought otherwise;
He threw the book and said, "Look you guys,
You bounced old Fred when you were up last time;
The tenth man stays, You're going with nine."

With tears in his eyes someone got off the load,
Threw his gear in the trunk and drove off down the road.
With thirty-six jumps he'd have probably done fine
But Fred would be happy if we got the first nine.

The Beech took off in a black smoke cloud
Just under the wires and over the crowd!
Spectators ducked and faces got white
And we didn't breathe 'til we were in flight!

We were two hours late when we hit twelve-five
And the pilot yelled with fear in his eyes,
"Get ready you guys, we're going on in
'Cause we're out of gas! Better check my pins!"

"Man in the door!" came a muffled shout,
I was tying my shoes when the base fell out;
The pin was gone, then three, then four,

And then there was nothing but me and the door!

I dove head low, someone's boot in my mouth;
The prop blast hit as I flew out;
Tumbling plane overhead, falling bodies below,
Stable at last, but a long way to go.

I tracked so hard that I couldn't stop,
My breath was gone and my eyeballs popped!
Drilled a hole in a cloud and started to flare,
And when I came out the star was there.

I got a good grip and the star was round;
One eye on the needle and one on the ground
We started to break when we heard a yell
And across from me was a face from hell!

Trailing red smoke from an M-18
A phantom tenth man appeared on the scene!
We wanted to break but found we could not.
Our grips froze tight when he hit the slot!

I'll swear to this day it was Flying Fred,
He had surplus gear and his eyes were red!
With a laugh you could hear and a wave of his hand
He broke off the star just over a grand!

Nobody waved and nobody tracked,
The trees got so big we just unpacked!
Reserves went by! Out flashed my own!
But that red smoke flew towards the ground

Out by the peas was the Federal Man
Timing low pulls with a watch in his hands.
Came the lowest pull of all that day
Because Phantom Fred was heading his way.

With a grinning laugh and a blast of wind
In a cloud of smoke Fred brought it on in!
Lightning flashed and thunder rolled!
When the smoke cleared away there was just a hole.

White reserves started landing there,
The Beech was down in a field somewhere
The F.A.A. didn't like all this;
The man staggered off to file a near miss.

We all looked at the hole, then we all shook hands.
It was legal now, our first ten-man.
Where Fred had gone we couldn't say
But our witness was the F.A.A.

That night over a beer we thought of a way
To salute Flying Fred's memorial day.
Where that smoke bomb hit, now a marker stands,
It says, "Boys, I was with you on your first ten-man!"

SKYDIVER

by George McCulloch

He who climbs into a plane
   And mounts into the blue,
Then dives to dare the Sea of Air,
   Has drunk the magic Brew.

Floating downward—swinging, turning—
   Creature now of earth and sky—
He has felt a deeper yearning,
   He has heard the eagle's cry.

Though his landing be with laughter—
   Though he seems like other men—
He will never—ever after—
   Be the same, again.

      *   *   *

He will circle higher, higher,
   Deafened by the engine's thunder.

SKYDIVING

He will watch the earth grow smaller,
    And will reach a world of wonder.

Up he climbs through snowy mountains—
    Cliffs and chasms, strangely near.
Look, below! The field, the hangars,
    And the target, sharp and clear.

Now the plane is on the jump-run,
    His heart is pounding fast . . .
The exit-point creeps nearer:
    And the Moment comes at last!

Cut! The engine's roar is muted . . .
    The prop-blast whips his face . . .
The MOMENT is upon him,
    And he plunges into space.

He is falling—farther, farther—
    Turning, diving, floating free;
Moving to the magic music
    Of an unseen symphony.

Soon the tiny cars seem larger
    On the highway far below;
. . . The seconds race, remorseless;
    The rooftops grow and grow.

Closer moves the hand, and closer
    To the "Sixty" on the "clock" . . .
Now it's "In!" to find that handle,
    And it's "A-ah"—the opening shock!

The great chute buds and blossoms,
    And he thanks the gods that be,
Like a sailor nearing harbor,
    Safe from perils of the sea.

His sail is full above him;
    He swings beneath its dome,

Then he seeks and finds the windline,
 And sets his course for home.

*   *   *

He who climbs into a plane,
 And mounts into the blue,
Then dives to dare the Sea of Air,
 Has joined the favored Few.

Though his landing be with laughter—
 Though he seem like other men—
He will never—ever after—
 Be the same, again.

He has climbed the cloudy Mountain—
 He has tasted of the fountain—
He will never—ever after—
 Be the same, again.

The Eternal Skydiver

by Lori Spring

Ninety-three million miles from the airport where Danny Erhardt was parking his car, something strange was happening. Another solar system had passed a little too close to ours—if you call a hundred light years close—and our sun was suffering greatly from near impact. Great masses of churning gases swirled over its surface and exploded into the atmosphere like a celestial fourth of July exhibition. Dust and solid bits of the sun also broke away and began to orbit.

The effects of the near miss of the solar systems were just beginning to be felt this bright blue Saturday morning. The weather was perfect, but yet there was a feeling in the air, almost like the calm before a storm.

Danny Erhardt was whistling "Off We Go Into The Wild Blue Yonder" as he unloaded his rigs and oxygen gear, and carried them to the parking area. Other jumpers noted that he seemed even happier than usual—if that was possible. Why shouldn't he be? He had been planning and saving and getting ready for today's jump for a long time!

Thirty grand! A whole new experience up where nothing flies but man, and all those beautiful minutes of free-fall awaiting him.

Cracking jokes all the while, and whistling bits of this and that, Danny packed his rig and checked out his protective clothing. He made sure the smoke holder was properly mounted on his boot and the spares handy, and then checked out his oxygen equipment. Though he didn't normally use one, Danny had attached a Sentinel to his reserve. After all, no one in the club had yet jumped from thirty thousand, and who knew what might happen on the way down. The Sentinel was set to open the chute at 3,500 feet, so it was really a last resort kind of thing and Danny was sure he wouldn't need it. After all, he was healthy as a horse, strong as a bull, and had almost 700 jumps in his log. He had never even dumped a reserve. Any trouble he got into, he could always get out of.

His sometime nickname was "Birdrock," affectionately given him by the other jumpers, who found he could work like a bird in the air or go into his own version of the delta and plunge like a rock. He had been in on more hookups and baton passes than anyone else in the Crofton Sky Gods, and had even invented several spectacular group stunts that made the club a favorite at fairs and air shows.

Other Sky Gods were showing the excitement of the day as they prepared for jumps higher than usual. Danny had obtained the services of an excellent pilot and a surplus B-25 military bomber. He was earning back some of its cost by taking a load to seventeen-five on his way up, and these people were busily planning what maneuvers they would try in the long free-fall.

It wasn't quite the same as an earthquake, and no one else even seemed to notice it, so Danny paid no attention to the tremor he felt in the ground and chalked it up to nerves. It wasn't like him to get the jitters, but this was a big day and the air was so still and no birds were singing, and it was almost time to go.

The high load was called and those going jostled and joked their way to the plane for pin check and a ground picture taken by someone's girlfriend. During the long ride to seventeen-five there was little kidding around, with only occasional jokes being cracked. Many cigarettes were smoked and several comments made about the increasing cold. Presently it was time for the spot and exit. Amid the pell-mell rush for the open bomb bay and the cries of "I'm John Wayne," "Bonzai" and "Geronimo," Danny felt strangely alone. Now there were only himself, the pilot and his co-pilot.

The climb to thirty grand took forever and Danny couldn't help checking his altimeter repeatedly. It was working beautifully. Of course. It was brand new and had cost a small fortune. Taking big drags on his oxygen, Danny Erhardt tried to quiet the growing uneasiness he felt. Nothing seemed to help, and just as he was about to panic and hang up the whole venture, the pilot signaled jump run. Suddenly calm, and unable to understand his previous agitation, Danny was very businesslike as he secured his bail-out oxygen and his smoke bomb, and prepared to make his spot. Good Lord, the DZ looked small down there. It seemed there was a haze in the air and he knew his spot would probably not be as accurate as he would have liked, but oh well, time to worry about that at ten grand when "Deadeye Dan, king of the trackers," would go into action.

Signaling for the cut, Danny took a deep breath and plunged into the cold, thin air. And there it was—that wonderful sense of freedom—that feeling of exhilaration—that always tingled through him in free-fall. Just to limber up, he did a nine second series in the weak air, and then gave vent to his joy in a string of great galloping back loops across the sky, trailing pink smoke behind. He hoped those below, especially the seventeen-five load, now on the ground, were watching and enjoying his jump as much as he.

They weren't.

At all.

He was the last thing on their minds at the moment. Their world was in trouble. BIG trouble.

The sun, still reeling from its near collision with the unknown star, reached its ultimate in destruction at that instant, and split in two. Both halves leaped out of their orbit and started off in different directions, leaving nine planets and assorted moons to tumble and stagger in pursuit of one or the other. The third planet from the destroyed sun gave a life-ending lurch and started after the larger of the two halves. Its moon was caught in a strange new gravity and began a plunge that would bury it in the continent of Africa and annihilate one third of what was once called Earth. There was no life any more. Only dust and shambles and some one-celled organisms in the puddles where oceans had been.

Having just failed to write his name in pink smoke down the sky, Danny bent to check his altimeter and found to his surprise and pleasure that he was still at 22,000 feet. Time sure went slow up here. He did a few more stunts and fitted another smoke bomb into his boot, going Z to do it. Tiring of barrel rolls and cartwheels, he stabled out and again checked his altimeter. What the devil—it now showed twenty grand. Impossible. A glance at his stop watch assured Danny that his altimeter was badly mistaken. He had been in the air far too long to have fallen only 10,000 feet. Great. Now he'd have to rely on vision alone. Where did he suppose he was? Land still looked awfully hazy and far away. Maybe he was goofing out for lack of oxygen. He took deep drags of it and found his head and vision no different. His altimeter was very different, however. It now registered 23,000 feet. Going backwards yet. Broootherrr. Something up here was sure going nuts, and Danny wasn't at all sure it was just the altimeter.

The Earth was looking smaller and smaller. But that was insane. Who ever heard of a drop zone running away from a skydiver? Some part of his brain told Danny to relax. Even a nut having hallucinations would hit the ground eventually. Thank God for the Sentinel. It would get him down all right. Just fall stable, take oxygen and wait.

His mind was so busy fighting down his panic that his eyes forgot to look around, and the next time Danny noticed his instruments, the stop watch told him he had been falling almost five minutes and the altimeter needle must have gone around again backwards because it was at 700 feet.

With a heat stopping bolt Danny suddenly realized that he could now look down and see the whole West Coast. Something was definitely bad wrong. The Earth was either moving away from him or he was falling upwards. He couldn't decide which of the two was the most impossible. The only thing he knew for sure was that he was running out of air and breath and that he was very alone.

In a terrible moment of realization he added up the strange weather, the ground tremors and the dust clouds below him, and he knew somehow everything was all over and he was doomed. Taking the last gulp from the oxygen bottle he cut it away, and with a strange calm, affixed his last smoke flare and went into his special Delta, aiming for a target he knew would not be there.

Hooking a thumb through the ripcord he knew he'd never pull, Danny Erhardt smiled his biggest smile, closed his eyes, and became the eternal skydiver.

The Man Who Flew Like a Bat*

by Martin Caidin

Red Grant is a little man in stature . . . but a big man in the courage department. He learned parachuting with the 507th Parachute Infantry in World War II and then got into it for profit sort of by accident. He began to jump for various air shows in the United States and Canada and had many narrow brushes with death. Red did all the air circus tricks you've heard about. He carried sacks of flour under his arms and released the flour behind him in huge contrails in a swooping pattern before popping open his chute; he rode the top wing of a biplane as it looped and rolled over the horrified crowds, and he stood up in a racing convertible and climbed a flimsy rope ladder up to a low-flying plane. But his one goal was to someday fly the bat wings. The bat wings are a 180-pound assemblage of nylon and wire that transforms the wearer into a human airplane; there are wings and webbing between the legs. A man can control his flight and perform spectacular free-fall maneuvers . . . but it's the most dangerous of all parachute techniques. Red learned to use the bat wings and become fairly proficient with them. Then he decided to try

---

* This is a true jump story—not fiction.

to pull off a real stunt: he would try to make the first international batwing flight . . . from the United States into Canada. The occasion was to be an air circus in Houlton, Maine. He figured it would be simple: just bail out with enough altitude to allow him to glide across the Canadian border, then parachute down. He made it easy. But the next jump, this time in Kentucky, was a different story. As he propelled himself out of the plane, he was brought up with a terrific jolt. Somehow his gear had fouled something on the way out and now he found himself hanging precariously from the bottom of the plane with the ground 10,000 feet below. How could he free himself? Was the pilot aware that he was still with him? . . .

In all the history of barnstorming, air shows and special air circuses, there have been only seventy-six *batmen*—and R. W. "Red" Grant, diminutive in stature but a giant in courage and skill, is the last of the breed. The batman is perhaps the most unusual of all the men and quickly becomes a human projectile that swoops, darts, turns, spirals, dives, and glides—until his arms almost begin to pop out of their sockets from the hammering pressure of the air against his special bat wings.

Clem Sohn, one of the veteran barnstormers in business before World War II, started the dangerous stunt back in 1935. Sohn was already famous for his long-delay drops from airplanes, and when he rigged up a set of home-built wings and sails to attach to his body, hurtling through the air like a huge bat or aerial manta ray, he proved to be an immediate crowd sensation. The proof was in the gate; dollar income soared wherever he appeared. In 1937 he took his wings to France. Parachuting in Europe before World War II was already a sport of great enthusiasm, and the Continentals had the habit of looking down their noses at parachuting in the United States. But the bat-winged Sohn proved an immediate smash hit. In a way he reached the peak of his career in France . . . .

He bailed out one afternoon before a packed crowd of several thousand Frenchmen. They went through the appropriate gasps and clutching of breasts in fright as Sohn started his batwinged glide toward the earth. Sohn jerked the ripcord of his main chute, and the crowd sat up straight and started rising to their feet when the silk streamered instead of cracking open in the full canopy. They were all on their feet and screaming when he deployed his reserve pack and that one streamered also. Both chutes fluttered behind him like two useless rags. Clem Sohn smashed into the ground at ninety miles per hour. The first spectators to run to the scene found a red pulp instead of a man; Sohn was very dead.

It was ten years later that Red Grant had occasion to think clearly of Clem Sohn. At that moment Grant, who said the vision of Sohn came to him like a flash, was plummeting toward the earth. And like Sohn, he also had trailing behind him two long, whistling, and very useless ribbons of silk. With some frantic maneuvering and handling of the shroud lines Grant managed to get a canopy open before he plunged into the earth to his death. Muses Red Grant:

"It's a miracle I'm still alive. Only a damn fool would have gotten into this business in the first place—a business I got into by accident.

"As most of you remember, the fall of 1945 was a crazy, mixed-up period. What was left of my outfit, the 507th Parachute Infantry, came back from the ETO to get paid off. I changed into civvies after seven years in the regular Army and immediately got into trouble.

"I went up to Denver to see a chick I had been more or less engaged to during the war. Killing time, I went into a typical soldier trap to have a beer. There was an argument going on at the bar. Some Services-of-Supply soldier was mouthing off at a B-girl, then he hit her. All five-feet-seven of me got up from the table and I went over and clipped that bird twice. He slumped out of sight. A low growl came from behind me— I had committed the cardinal sin of hitting a *soldier*. Some more rear-echelon commandos came from nowhere and I high-tailed it out of there and went flying up the street. I caromed off three guys who grabbed me and yelled, "Whoa there, little man!" I looked up at three bruisers wearing the patch of the 82nd Airborne on their shoulders. I knew them all, so we went back and cleaned out the bar. Afterwards we went up to my hotel room and toasted Fightin' Slim Jim Gavin with three fifths of Old Joyful.

"Next day, I cleaned up and went to see my fiancee. She was downright cool, and I didn't get the drift until I saw her flicking her eyes back and forth from me to the picture on the mantle. it was taken in London, and I looked like a Mexican general: white silk scarf, fruit salad down to there, the fourragere—the works. When she told me she couldn't possibly introduce me to her friends until I put on my uniform, boots and ribbons, I walked out the door and haven't seen her since.

"I had no job, no fiancee, no prospects. Soldiering was all I knew. I was used to living under pressure, never knowing from one day to the next whether I would get killed or be doing the killing. Most of the guys who came out of the greatest adventure of them all settled down; a few of us weren't ready to face the same desk day after day. For me, there was always that next hill to climb . . . ."

It was the end of the First World War all over again. Then Red Grant, through dating another chick, ended up at a meeting of the Civil Air Patrol in Denver. He fidgeted while the meeting went on; the CAP was getting together an air show. Grant's ears perked up a bit when he heard the words "parachute jumper," and the next moment everyone heard from his date the Red Grant *was* a jumper. He agreed to their request to make a jump at the air show. Red's girl would provide the transportation herself: she would fly a beat-up old PT-23 trainer. With something interesting happening for the first time since he came back stateside, he went out and rented a full jumper's rig.

"It wasn't until I was alone in my hotel room that night," admits Red, "that I realized I didn't know a damn thing about free-fall; all of my combat jumps had been static-line drops from C-47's. I was worried about it all night.

"There was nothing to it. Alice got the PT-23 up to three thousand feet and I stepped out on the narrow wing and went off into space, keeping my left hand over my head to act as a rudder. The landing strip rushed up to meet me, I pulled the D-ring, my bones were wrenched by the shock of the chute opening, then I landed on the runway standing up. The crowd roared—and I had just made fifty bucks."

Red jumped again that afternoon; this time, however, he pulled the D-ring just a bit too late, missed his target, and almost plowed into the grandstand. He was gathering up the folds of the parachute when a woman approached him.

"How many free-falls have you made?" she asked.

"You just saw the first two," Red admitted candidly.

"Well, you stupid so-and-so," she said easily, "if you live a year jumping like that you'll be lucky. But if you do live, you'll be one of the best."

Red stared open-mouthed at her. That was his introduction to Fay Cox, whom he calls "America's greatest female parachutist."

At the end of the day, Red Grant had made one hundred dollars and decided he had just started on a new career. He began to jump for different air shows throughout the United States and Canada. He went through one minor disaster after another, but always avoided major injury. He stresses with candor:

> I knew cold fear. In Valley City, North Dakota, on Labor Day of 1948, I went out of a Super Cub at 8,000 feet in a freshening wind. I fell through space until I could smell the earth, then I pulled the ripcord handle. Nothing happened. I pulled with both hands and the handle came off, leaving the ripcord still in the housing. It can't happen, but it did, and I was hurtling toward the earth with a useless ripcord in my hand and a stupid look on my face.
>
> I went for the reserve chute and frantically threw handfuls of silk away from me. I was on my back when the chute popped and it felt like I had kicked myself in the back with my heels. I looked up and saw to my horror that I had a double Mae West—four small puffs of silk instead of one big one—and that three panels had blown. I tried to work the fouled lines off the tops of the reserve canopy, but they stayed fast and the silk began ripping to shreds. I was still struggling with the lines when the earth rushed up and slammed into me. The air was smashed from my lungs and then somebody turned out the lights.
>
> I woke up ten minutes later in a field covered with boulders the size of my head. Ripped silk was all over the place. That little angel sitting on my shoulder had saved my life. No bones were broken, but by late that night I had turned a sickly shade of yellow-green from my neck to my ankles. When I heard the taped playback of the radio announcer's hysterical description of my fall and probable death, the reaction hit me and my legs gave way—it was the nearest I ever came to fainting.

Undaunted by his brushes with death, Red Grant added new gimmicks to his act. He was a natural crowd-pleaser, the kind of man who forms one of the major elements of any air circus. He leaped from airplanes—or rather, just fell out of them—with open bags of flour beneath each arm. It is an extremely difficult way to sustain a long freefall, since the jumper has no opportunity and lacks the means of stabilizing his plunge. Notwithstanding the kind of problem that would give a sky diver the screaming horrors, Red plunged from high with the flour streaming from the two sacks, with his "twin flour contrails" weaving a pattern through the sky. By changing body position and the angle of his legs he actually achieved a controlled descent. Finally he tossed aside the bags, which fluttered behind him like falling moths, and jerked open his chute.

Red was much more than a stunt jumper. Like other stunt men he rode the top wing of a powerful Stearman, especially rigged for air show work, secured to "that bucking bronco only by straps on my feet and thin cables kept taut by locking my knees together." Like Frank Clarke, Tommy Walker and many of the great barnstormers, he stood up in a convertible and leaped aboard a rope ladder dangling from an airplane that passed overhead. Despite the variety of "gimmicks" he added to his routine, he kept inching toward what he wanted most of all—jumping the batwings.

It was in Jackson, Mississippi, that the crowd—the "pack of jackals"—finally drank its blood, and Red Grant got his batwings. As he recalls the day:

> I went on early in the show, jumped and free-fell a long way while three ships weaved around my flight path, wrapping me in great swaths of smoke. I touched down gently and sat on the grass to watch Billy Fisher wring out his little Ross Parakeet.... Billy taxied out, swung into the wind and shoved the throttle forward. The burst of power shot the Parakeet into the air like a rocket. He rolled, half-rolled and snap-rolled just off the deck. Then Billy pushed the nose up and got up to 1,200 feet and leveled off. The nose dropped straight down and the shriek of his engine tore apart the sky. At 800 feet the sound of the engine changed key and a puff of smoke erupted from the cowling. The nose came up sharply in a high g-load maneuver and the engine ripped loose from the mounts and hurtled backward

through the cabane struts. Parts of the upper left wing tore off and fluttered away in the slipstream. I was on my feet yelling to Billy to get out. I saw him stand up in the cockpit, then settle back in the bucket. The plane did a crazy kind of flat turn and skidded drunkenly away from the thousands of people in the stands below. The Parakeet half-rolled and went in inverted. Fisher was killed instantly.

The M.C. stayed on the mike and kept the crowd from smashing through the barriers to get at the wreckage and a few bloody souvenirs. Then he asked me to ride the top wing of the Stearman to get the crowd's mind off the tragedy. I secured the cables, the pilot revved up the engine and we took off. It was the most horrible moment of my life when we climbed out over the wreckage of Billy's plane. I looked down past my feet at the pilot and saw unashamed tears streaming under the rubber rims of his goggles.

After four years of working air shows I finally got my batwings. . . our regular batman came up to me and said, "Red, I've had it. The equipment is all yours." Then he walked away. I stood there wondering if that was the way I would wind up—defeated by too many women and too much booze before I was thirty-five.

I looked at the equipment I had inherited with two feelings: pride and fear. There was a lot of tradition behind those wings, and there was a lot of built-in danger.

You get in the wings like pulling on a pair of pants, except the pants are like webbing, stretched between the legs. The wings start at the ankle and go out at an angle almost to shoulder height. The wings are supported at the top by heavy round wooden poles, which are gripped with each hand halfway down the length so you can control the the flight attitude. The whole rig is permanently attached and can't be ditched in flight if something goes haywire. The wings go on over the regular jumpsuit, along with the main chute and the reserve, which hangs halfway down in front. An altimeter is attached to the reserve pack.

Including the boots and buffet hat and oversized goggles, the whole rig weighs 180 pounds. Bear in mind that I'm a small guy, tipping the scales at 140. Once I'm clear of the ship I am a human airfoil, prey to the laws of flight. But there is no engine for power, and only sheer endurance keeps the wings taut and at the proper attitude.

Red made his first batwing jump in August of 1949. He was scheduled to go into his act immediately after the comedy routine performed by Gloria Lynch. Gloria at twenty-four years of age was only four feet six inches tall, as pert and cute as a new button. She dressed in a pinafore and wore her hair in pigtails and looked exactly like a little girl—instead of one of the best female pilots in the flying business. Her act called for her to skip up to the announcer and beg for a ride in an airplane. Finally, with a carefully worked-out routine, she won the sympathy of the crowd and the announcer "gave in." He summoned a pilot, and Gloria went out to a biplane where she was strapped into the front seat. As the pilot started to the rear seat Gloria slapped home the throttle. She staggered into the air with a chorus of shrieks and horrified screams from the audience who were convinced that they were about to see the little girl killed. On his first day as a batman, Red was circling high over the field, waiting for Gloria Lynch to finish her act before he jumped.

He watched the little biplane far below him, dragging the field and roller-coasting in its mock landing attempts. Then something went wrong. An updraft snatched at the airplane, whisked away its lift and left it helpless in the air. The ship plunged into the field. Red's pilot side-slipped out of the sky like a bomb as he banged down to a landing. The two men ran from their ship to the crumpled wreckage just as rescuers were pulling Gloria from the cockpit.

She was a lot shorter now. Both feet had been torn off at the ankles.

Red's debut was postponed; the tragedy to Gloria overshadowed any "the show must go on" routine. Nobody wanted to fly any more that day.

Finally he jumped the wings. Wisely he paid strict attention to everything that happened and swiftly gained great skill with his bat gear. "Then," he explains, as confidence began to override natural caution, "I became confident enough to think I could pull off one of the biggest damnfool stunts ever dreamed up in aerial show business. Nobody had ever made an international batwing flight, and I elected myself to be the first man to try."

Red planned to make the big attempt when the circus made its showing in Houlton, Maine. The idea was for him to bail out with enough altitude to cross the border into Canada, glide to a safe landing area, crack his chute, and land. He picked his possible touchdown sites carefully, the newpapers played it up big, and the gate grew in leaps and bounds. The promoters were delighted.

The day before the jump Red decided to rest easy and went off to Presque Isle to loaf. He missed two boys who had hustled to the field to get the batman's autograph. The kids asked Rod Joclyn, one of the circus pilots, where the batman could be found. Rod told them that Grant had flown off, but would be back later. He told the kids to wait by the corner of the hangar.

"Now, he'll be flying high and fast when he comes," Rod explained carefully, "so you'll have to listen close to hear the birdlike noises he makes in flight." The kids waited till sundown gazing up into the sky with their hands cupped by their ears.

Despite the hullabaloo raised about Red Grant's international bat flight, show business demanded a lot of work before he would go into his climax. First he did his long free-fall, with two smoke planes writhing earthward about him. What happened on his next act nearly canceled out the ballyhooed stunt. He was to go through the bit of standing on the wing while the pilot jostled the airplane about. Red explained:

> We were going to do this one in an Argo, a biplane built in late 1918. They had wisely manufactured no more than nineteen of these beasts. I climbed up on the top wing, secured the thin cables and got ready for the takeoff. The pilot was feeling frisky as hell and turned that old biplane every way but loose. It's cold, windy and lonesome up there on the wing, and when the pilot starts violent acrobatics, the world goes insane: sky, earth and horizon whirl crazily, blending together in a mash of colors. The blast of the wind from the prop wash threatens to tear me loose from my slender moorings and fling me backward into space.
>
> The pilot decided to give us all a little extra thrill, he stalled out at the top of a loop and the plane fell off into a vicious spin. We did about five turns before he leveled off and dragged the field. My knees were weak when we landed, and when one of the cables holding me to the wing snapped, I fell straight back and wedged my butt in the windscreen. I was stuck fast, my legs dangling on either side of the fuselage. Somebody came out with tools and cut the windscreen apart so I could get free. Somehow, I lost all confidence in that pilot...."

Fifteen minutes later Red bundled and strapped into his cumbersome gear, jammed into the seat beside the pilot of a Piper Tri-Pacer, and climbed steeply for his X in the sky where he would shove himself out of the airplane and begin his long glide to Canada. But first there was that climb to altitude, and of all the things a jumper dislikes the most, it's waiting while an airplane sticks its nose into the sky and drags itself away from the earth. The jumper has nothing to do but sit. And when you're bundled into your gear and jammed into an airplane, that sitting means thinking, and a swift train of thoughts rumbles through your mind. It's not clear thinking; the man with the chutes on his back sweats out the climb by trying hard to concentrate on his procedure for the bailout. There are mental pictures of falling away from the airplane, of body movements, then a swift scan of the landing area, not seen in a static position, but expanding steadily and rapidly. On his way to altitude, Red offered himself silent congratulations on not having eaten before taking off.

"I figure that if I get clobbered," he explains, "the time the docs save in pumping out my stomach can be put to better use saving my neck."

By the time the Tri-Pacer has leveled off, Red has noticed:

> My hands are getting cold. In a few minutes they are like lumps of ice. I look at the altimeter, we are at 14,600 feet and I am not wearing gloves. It's easier to feel the ripcord with my bare hands, but nearly three miles up it's freezing cold. Then I see the signal far below—a car circling slowly on the runway. It's time to go.
>
> I look down and pick out the clump of trees I have selected as my jump point. The right wheel blocks the trees from sight and I reach over and hit the pilot on the shoulder and scream, "Chop it!" The pilot cuts back the throttle and I place my hands on either side of the door and propel myself backward clearing the struts. The Tri-Pacer shoots forward away from me, the sound of its engine is quickly lost in the rush of air past my head. I am on my back, staring up at the sky, my wings extended. My arms quiver with the strain and I am chilled clear through.
>
> *Snap!* I half-roll out automatically with a sharp wrench and am now flat and stable—a true winged projectile hurtling steeply and swiftly through the sky. There is no sound except the whistling of the wind and the popping of loose fabric on my jump suit. My

eyes search the earth, seeking the swath cut through the woods that marks the border. I see it a little to the left, and raise my right arm slightly to bank in that direction. I cross the border at 8,000 feet and—for the benefit of the crowd behind me at the airport—bank steeply and execute a 360-degree turn to let them know I made it.

I am down to 5,000 feet, peering ahead to spot the cleared areas chosen the day before. I see one, then another and another. But 5,000 feet is too high to pull, and I keep going. My arms are beginning to feel the strain of the long glide. Approaching the next cleared area I realize I can't hold out much longer and start a series of ever-steepening spirals that will get me down quickly. A thousand feet over the deck I pull the rip cord. My body is wrenched violently and I see champagne bubbles rising up before my eyes. Thank God there is no crosswind, for I am too exhausted to fool around with the shroud lines. The ground rushes up and I land with a bone-jarring thump.

Too beat to rise, I lie on the ground letting the cool breeze wash over my eyes. I stay flat on my back for ten minutes, waiting for the recovery team. Then I hear a jeep coming through the woods in low-low gear.

Newsmen inveigled the customs officials of Canada and the United States to grab Red from the Canadian and American sides of his anatomy, his legs straddling the border, and pretended to be fighting over him. Red went along with the publicity tug-of-war over his body and made the front pages throughout the entire area. Back at the airport from where he took off 25,000 people gave him a standing ovation.

Later, pilots estimated that Red Grant had flown the wings over a ground distance of four miles, while dropping less than three miles—a new record for the world.

Red was immensely pleased with his jump from the United States into Canada, but a short time later he was reminded once again—in the most ominous fashion possible—that every jump is a new leap straight into the jagged maw of unpredictable danger. He went out of a Cessna L-19 flown by a Kentucky Air National Guard pilot. Red always faced the problem of never knowing from what type of plane he would bail out, and the L-19 chilled him to the quick. Its door was narrow and confined and it seemed nothing but trouble in respect to making an exit with all his gear in a high wind. But the show was on, no other planes were available, and Red clambered into his seat. Then the pilot, a young lieutenant, strapped himself into the front seat, and secured his body with a new type of shoulder harness. The harness was secured with a cable that ran inside the cockpit from the belly of the ship and linked to an inertial system that provided limited freedom of movement. The L-19 dashed down the runway into the wind for no more than seventy feet and leaped into the air, hanging on its prop and scrabbling for the sky. At 10,000 feet the lieutenant leveled off and eased back on the throttle. Then Red got ready—

They signaled from the ground to *go!* and I unbuckled the seat belt and strained to heave myself up in a semi-upright position so I could get out of the door. I felt like a Labrador retriever trying to get out of a sardine can. I couldn't make it facing the door, so I worked myself around so my back could go out first. I gave the pilot the signal to chop the throttle, then heaved myself out into the blast of the slipstream.

I was brought up short with a wrenching jolt. Oh, my God! *I had fouled my gear on something!* I dangled underneath the belly of the airplane, unable to move. My first thought was, can the pilot keep the plane stable? He *had* to—my job was to free myself from whatever it was that locked me to the airplane.

I looked up and saw that the handgrip on my right wing was caught on the cable that ran underneath the belly of the ship. The lieutenant had told me the cable was stressed for 2,500 pounds, so breaking it was out of the question.

I reached for the cable, but missed it by inches; the terrific buffeting from the wind was bouncing me around like a wet rag. I tried for the landing gear, but the wind pressure blew me backward. I flapped there under the belly of the ship, completely helpless.

It was getting harder to draw air into my lungs, and I remembered that a trooper at Fort Bragg the year before had got hung up like I was and died before they could untangle his harness. I beat on the belly of the plane to let the pilot know I was still there. Then to my horror I began to oscillate back and forth under the landing gear. I saw that each swing brought me closer to the wheels. I made countless frantic grabs for the wheels, missing each time. With each miss, I

Jumpers closing into star formation. The jumper approaching the star appears to be sitting up to begin the last docking maneuvers necessary for a good entry. (Ray Cottingham photo)

felt panic rising inside me. I fought it down. After an eternity, I managed to grab one of the rubber tires and hung on, fighting the blast from the prop.

I heaved myself up a few inches and looked straight into the anxious face of the pilot. He cut back the throttle and yelled, "Can you pull yourself back into the plane?"

"Negative! Negative!"

The pilot unbuckled his harness and reached across the right-hand seat, stretching his right arm outward while keeping his left hand on the control column. That scared me as much as anything. I could just see him grabbing my hand and me pulling him out there with me—a great act, with both of us hanging from the landing gear, but what would we do for an encore?

"It won't work!" I screamed. "Try to pull me up there!" But he couldn't hear me. I groped upward, trying to reach the door, but the hurricane of wind whipped me back. I felt real despair and was sure we were both going to die.

What was he doing now? A strap whipped out from the door and almost hit me in the face. I reached for it and missed. I tried again. Failure. Once more, and I had it. I pulled myself painfully upward and shifted my weight, hoping to lessen the pressure that locked me to the cable. Up, up, up.

Suddenly I was free.

I fell away from the plane and fought down an instinct to pull the rip cord. I kept falling through space until I caught a flash of sunlight glinting from a pond. The thought passed through my mind: *If I don't pull, I'm going to get wet!* I yanked the rip cord.

The shock of the opening jerked me upright in the harness, and the sight of that orange-and-white canopy billowing above my head was the most beautiful thing I had ever seen.

I owe my life to the coolness of that pilot. He could have panicked and gone over the side with his chute, leaving me to my fate in the sky. But he didn't, he stuck it out and I was allowed to live.

Red Grant didn't learn until later just how much he really did owe to that young lieutenant in the front seat. When Red's weight snagged on the cable, the officer was slammed back in in his seat and immobilized. He zipped open his flight suit and shrugged it off his shoulders.

Red stared at two deep, bleeding grooves where the cables had sawed back and forth through the pilot's flesh when Grant had started to oscillate. The lieutenant, who was in agony during Red's own torment, would carry those scars the rest of his life.

Peak Experience at 6:45 A.M.*

by Michael Horan

I knew when the alarm was set that 5 o'clock in the morning would come all too soon and that it would be a hard deadline for me to meet. I was right. Not really wanting to believe what was happening, I staggered to my feet as a very ingratiating alarm had ended my peaceful dreams.

After a quick shower and an even quicker bite to eat, I loaded my parachute gear into the car and headed over to Pete Krieg's house. Pete had called the night before and offered me a chance to jump out of his hot-air balloon the next morning, and from a pretty high altitude. The chances of actually getting to jump out of his balloon seemed pretty remote to me. About this time of morning all I could think of was how warm my electric blanket had been. The sun wasn't up yet, but I could tell the weather wasn't too great. The morning was foggy, and a pretty good layer of scud covered Indianapolis, threatening to rain anytime. At any rate, I was already up and figured what the hell, might as well give it a go.

Pete and I had been talking about making a high jump out of his balloon for some time now, but this early in the morning seemed a little ridiculous. However, the prospect of actually making the jump intrigued me into action. I was starting to get awake and already could feel the twinges of anticipation creep into my body. Driving up to Pete's house made me feel somewhat more confident. There were several members of the chase crew hanging around the garage where Pete kept his 8,000 cubic foot AX-8 homemade balloon. After a few quick hello's, we all went into the house and devoured some coffee and doughnuts. Ruth, Pete's wife, Anita Harrell, Dave Menchofer, Jon Pavey, and Doug DeArmond, all members of the chase crew, were pretty used to this early morning schedule. Anita told me the idea was to launch the balloon as the sun is rising, when there is little or no wind. Seemed like a pretty good idea to me, and fairly soon we all loaded into several cars and made a caravan to the Lion's

* This is a true jump story—not fiction.

Park in Zionsville, where the launch was to be made. The time was still an unbelievable 5:40 a.m.

Anita rode with me on the way, so we naturally started talking about the morning activities. I was awake somewhat, but my mind wasn't really functioning too well when she asked: "How come you want to jump out of that perfectly good balloon?" Feeling somewhat caught off guard, I just replied a weak, "Why not?" Philosophizing I normally don't mind, but at this hour of the morning I just couldn't get into it. So we just let the matter drop and discussed other matters as we drove to Zionsville.

The weather still looked terrible, and in fact, the closer we got to the park the more it looked like it was going to rain. Just what I needed. However, the weather didn't seem to bother these hearty balloonists at all. Immediately upon arriving they all got busy and started unloading the balloon. Their enthusiasm got me worked up again, and pretty soon all of us were involved in setting up. About that time, Dave Theil arrived. Dave was to be Pete's co-pilot during this little experience, which also served as a semi-annual check ride for Pete.

Occasionally a little patch of blue would peek through the clouds and give us some hope, then close up. So we just waited, and talked about the plans for the ascent and jump. It was agreed that if the chase crew lost the balloon or the jumper, we were all to call back to Pete's house and give our location. Sounded great. Marginal weather forced us to make early morning small talk. Fortunately someone had brought a thermos of coffee, and that gave us something to do.

After a quick trip to the bushes, I returned to find a frenzy of activity keeping everyone busy. A fairly large blue opening in the sky got us all involved in inflating the balloon. Much to my amazement and morale, it was time to get my rig on and get with the program.

The balloon was inflated, and Pete was shouting orders to get ready. Pete got in the basket, followed by Dave and then me. A strange sensation crept into my body. I had the distinct feeling this was going to be one hell of a good treat. The time was 6:45 a.m., and my Peak Experience was just starting as the three of us slowly lifted off the ground.

The noise from the butane burners was deafening as the

8-man paired "in-out" formation (photo courtesy of The Golden Knights)

balloon ascended through the layer of low hanging scud. For about a thousand feet our vision was partially obscured. At 1,500 feet we broke through and entered a beautiful bright blue world. The sun was just rising and for miles all we could see were soft and rolling white puffy clouds that practically hypnotized the three of us. Pete was busy regulating the ascent rate with burners, Dave was into taking pictures, and I was just soaking in the good vibes. Leaning on the side of the basket and gazing at the new day was enough for me. When Pete turned off the burners from time to time, the silence was perfect. We were three men, free from the earth, at least for the time being.

The balloon was slowly drifting towards the northeast and climbing about 500 to 700 feet per minute. The rising sun had burned off most of the ground haze, permitting us to see the ground clearly. By this time we were miles from Zionsville and about 10,000 feet high. It was about time for my non-participating role to end. I sensed a familiar tingle in my body at the prospect of actually making the jump.

We hadn't talked about it, but Dave wanted to know how I was going to exit the balloon. When I told him I was going off backwards, it brought a chuckle from him, and Pete mumbled something about sky divers which I didn't try to absorb. We were now at 13,300 feet AGL, and my big opportunity was here. Grabbing the support ropes of the balloon, I managed to balance myself on the edge of the basket. Dave took some pictures, and Pete told me not to forget some Indian's name as I jumped. As I leaned over backwards and looked down, my heart began pounding as the adrenalin started to flow. My feelings were weird and difficult to describe, but I felt alive.

Waiting for a few seconds heightened my anxiety. And then, leaning backwards I literally fell off the basket head over heels from the nearly motionless balloon.

Now I was one who was free from all earthly ties except gravity. Tumbling out of control produced some novel sensations for a few seconds. I could actually feel myself falling, as if from a high diving board or from a high cliff. This sensation gradually gave way to yet another feeling that was completely different from an airplane jump. Falling faster and faster toward terminal velocity became a very intense experience. Picking up speed through the complete progression involved in attaining terminal velocity was a first time experience. Gradually, after about eight seconds, the experience became more like a normal jump. These fleeting sensations lasted but a few seconds but gave me plenty to think about during the rest of the 60-second-plus delay.

I continued falling during the early morning hours just enjoying the descent. It has been a long time since I had enjoyed a jump without having to worry about the spot, making circles, turning style, or doing an accuracy jump. The beauty and solitude were exhilarating.

After landing on the interchange between Interstate I-69 and Indiana 37, all I could do was to take a few minutes to catch my breath and soak in the experience just lived. Still flushed with excitement, I decided not to try and make sense out of my feeling. None was really called for, so I decided to forego analysis until a later date.

All-woman 15-member Penta Wedge (Ray Cottingham photo)

Fortunately I had landed near a John Deere farm implement store that was nearby and open. Within a half hour I had called in my position to Pete's wife, packed my rig, and answered the big question asked by one of the employees: "How come you jumped out of that balloon?" His question had a familiar ring to it. I told him as forthrightly as possible it was just for fun, and I really felt relieved when the chase car arrived and whisked me away. About an hour later after retrieving the balloon, we were all sitting in a restaurant feeding our hungry faces.

Dave calculated the balloon had traveled approximately 24 air miles, and the elapsed time from lift off to touchdown was one hour and 48 minutes. Everyone agreed what great fun the whole thing had been. Pete and Dave talked about being able to hear me fall away from the balloon in the still

A standard part of demonstration jumps: a Golden Knights team member with the US flag and a smoke grenade on his boot. (Photo courtesy of The Golden Knights)

morning air. It had reminded them of a sonic scream: very loud and really fast.

During the course of the meal, Anita wanted me to tell what my feelings were about the jump. Everyone waited for my response. In a moment of inspiration I said the entire sequence was a Peak Experience and was therefore difficult to explain and even more difficult to describe. I suggested the only real way of knowing what it felt like was to make a jump out of a balloon. Then they would know what I knew. I went back to my scrambled eggs, Anita ordered another coffee, and Pete mumbled something about sky divers.

THE SKY ABOVE, THE THUD BELOW DEPT.

One of America's fast-growing "fun" sports is "Sky-Diving". Nothing beats the thrill of leaping from a plane and floating through the air. And if you're lucky enough to be wearing a parachute, you can even do it more than once! In order to familiarize himself with this popular new sport, a member of the MAD Staff actually took up "Sport Parachuting" and tried many dives. His favorites are "Hurley's" in Rockefeller Center, and "Rick's" on Third Avenue. But we've gotten him to come out of these dives long enough to present:

A MAD LOOK AT SKY DIVING

FIRST, LET'S TAKE A LOOK AT THE THRILL OF "SKY-DIVING"...

You stand in the doorway of the plane, the wind rushing by your face. It's your first jump, but you're strangely calm.

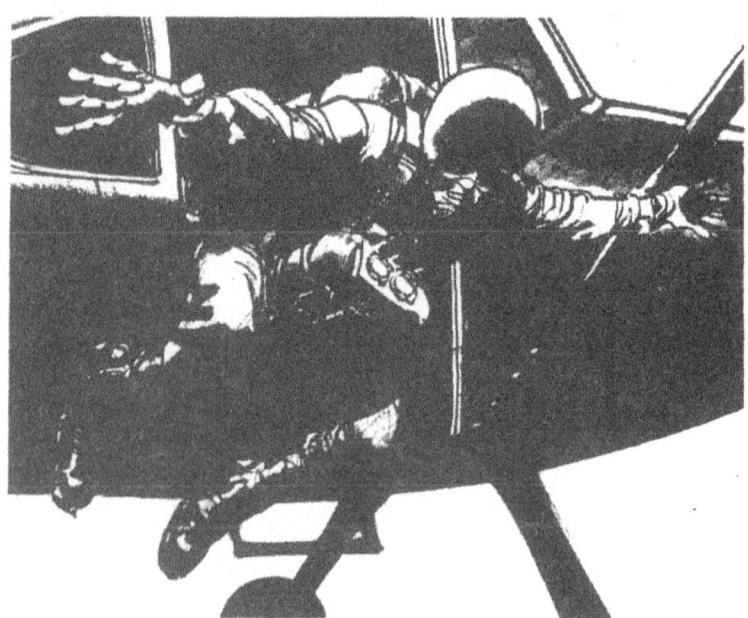

You gaze down at the ground far below you . . . and then you leap . . . out into space . . . out into the rushing wind . . .

All your Instructor's words about "the landing fall" come back to you. You look up at the horizon . . . you relax . . .

. . . you plummet Earthward . . . and make a perfect landing! Now if you can only do it once the plane is off the ground!

WRITER: DICK DE BARTOLO   ARTIST: JACK DAVIS

NOW THAT YOU KNOW WHAT THE THRILL IS LIKE,
LET'S TAKE A CLOSER LOOK AT . . .

SKY-DIVING EQUIPMENT

HELMET
The function of the Helmet is quite obvious. It protects the ground from the shock of your head—should you by chance make an incorrect landing upside down.

GOGGLES
Goggles come in clear plastic or assorted tints, and protect your eyes from wind and glare. For Novice Sky-Divers, they also come with "The Lord's Prayer" printed on the inside of the lenses.

MAIN BACK PACK
The Main Back Pack contains a fully-steerable Sport Parachute (or sometimes just wads of newspaper — if you Sky-Dive with "funny" friends.)

JUMP SUIT
The Jump Suit is worn over your regular clothes to afford less wind-resistance, and to protect them from dust, dirt, water and mainly...nausea.

RESERVE CHUTE
If for any reason the Main Chute does not open, there is something the Sky-Diver can do—besides screaming and crying and watching his whole life flash before his eyes. He activates his Reserve Chute which, although unsteerable, will get him back to Earth safely. (If you can call landing in an active volcano or a pool of quicksand or a large chimney or shark-infested water—safely!)

This is your instructor talking! I've decided that you're not ready to jump!

JUMP BOOTS
Jump Boots with heavy soles are worn to cushion the shock of landing, but care must be taken as to the thickness of these soles. Too thin soles will pass more shock to the body, and too thick soles will bounce the Diver back into the plane.

RADIO TRANSMITTER
A compact Radio Receiver is usually carried by the Novice Sky-Diver so that his Instructor can communicate with him once he has left the plane.

NOW THAT YOU KNOW THAT THE EQUIPMENT IS LIKE, LET'S TAKE A CLOSER LOOK AT ...

THE JUMP

In preparation for the Jump, the Jumpmaster will first release a "Streamer" which falls and drifts at approximately the same rate of speed as the Parachutist. By observing this "Streamer", the Jumpmaster can calculate the correct exit point so the Sky-Diver will land right on the "Target". For example:

SPOTTING

A. Streamer is dropped from plane over Target.
B. Streamer lands ½ mile downwind of Target.

C. To compensate, plane goes ½ mile upwind of Target, and Diver exits.
D. But diver lands three miles upwind of Target, as wind has shifted!

EXITING

There are two methods of leaving the plane. The first one is called "The Poised Exit" in which the Novice pushes off from the aircraft and goes into the Spread-Eagle position.

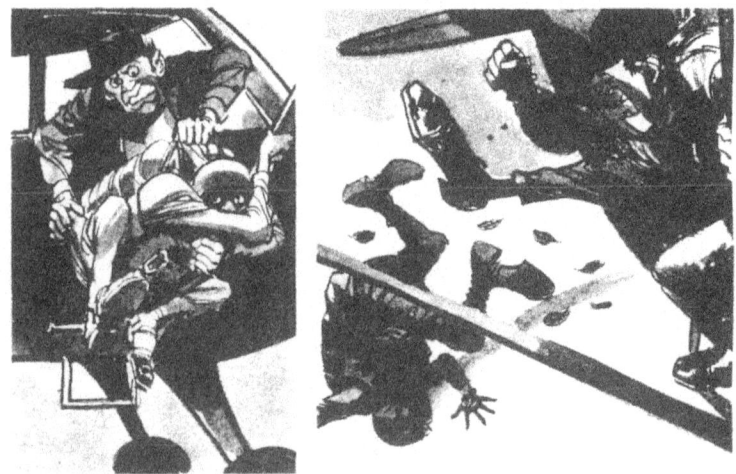

The second one is called "The Not-So Poised Exit" in which the Novice is forcibly ejected from the aircraft . . . mainly by the Instructor, who cannot tolerate "Chicken" students!

FALLING

You're in the air now . . . and as you float Earthward in a Spread-Eagle Free-Fall, you dream of far-away places . . .

. . . and well you should! Mainly because you're just about to be sucked into a Boeing 707 Jet on its way to Japan!

OPENING THE CHUTE

Chutes can be opened in one of two ways. The Advanced Student will use the "Rip Cord"—and open the Chute when he wishes . . .

. . . preferably, before making contact with the ground!

The Novice will rely on the "Static Line"—a line which is attached inside the plane and automatically opens the Chute as the Diver falls away. See the smile on this Novice's face as the "Static Line" grows taut and yanks his Chute open—

See the smile disappear as he realizes the "Static Line" has also yanked the Chute off his back. But this Novice isn't worried. That's why he has a "Back-Up" Chute! And that's exactly where it is—"back up" there on the plane!

MANEUVERING THE CHUTE

Sport Parachutes can actually be steered by using the turning devices or special openings located on either side of the canopy. These turning devices are connected by suspension lines to the harness.

Pull down on the right suspension line and you'll enjoy the sensation of seeing your parachute turn right.

Now pull down on the left suspension line and you'll enjoy the sensation of seeing your parachute turn left.

Don't pull down on *both* suspension lines or you'll enjoy the sensation of seeing your parachute from above.

CALCULATING THE "FREE-FALL"

The more advanced Sky-Diver will begin to make lengthy "Free-Falls" before opening his Parachute. In order to do this, there are calculations to be made to determine at what altitude and at what split-second the Chute should be opened. For this purpose, the advanced Parachutist carries a combination "Altimeter–Stop Watch" affixed to his Reserve Chute. Note how critical these calculations can be:

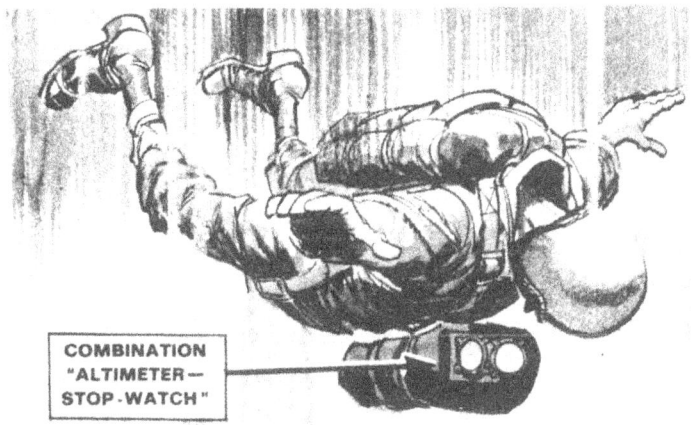

This diver has made calculations for a 9000-foot Free-Fall.

Too bad the ground was actually only 8500 feet below him!

LANDING

Let's assume that you have made the right calculations and you've opened your Chute before reaching the ground. Now you must prepare for the "PLF" or "Parachute Landing Fall" in order to avoid "TBL" or "Two Broken Legs". As you touch down, you "fall" along the side of your body—either right or left. In this way, the shock is divided among your feet, calves, thighs, buttocks, and whatever other part of your body happens to hit the ground . . . usually your wristwatch.

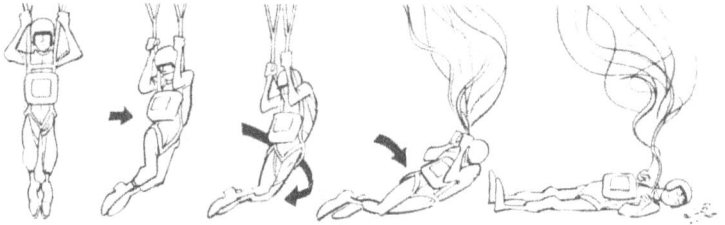

The beginner can practice this by jumping from a three-foot-high stool or step. After he's mastered that, he can jump from a plane, land on any three-foot-high stool or step, and take it from there!

SAFETY CHECKS

Before a Jump, every piece of equipment should be checked by a trained Professional Instructor. Note that Instructor in picture below is "feeling" to see if Student is wearing his Parachute correctly. (Instructors normally can "see" if Student is wearing his Parachute correctly, but this Professional has his helmet on backwards, blocking his vision.)

SAFETY RECORD

Did you know that "Sport Parachute Jumping" is safer than driving? See the man in the wreck on the highway below? He was on his way to a Sky-Diving Center when he hit a tree while avoiding a Chutist who had landed in the road ahead.

*Their record in skydiving
may never be surpassed
This is the story of Al
Krueger and his team.
You may know them better as . . .*

Captain Hook and the Sky Pirates

Leaders in the Sport

If you think of it in terms of professional football, the story would go like this: you, as a leader, assemble a team, build it to national potential, take it through a winning season to the Super Bowl . . . and lose. But with essentially the same players, again take the team through the playoffs and win—and again—and again, for a third year. To the Super Bowl and victory. Unheard of—in professional football. But in skydiving terms, that's the story of Al Krueger and the Sky Pirates.

And skydiving may never have a team capable of surpassing the achievements of Captain Hook's crew.

Al Krueger attended schools in Bellflower, a Los Angeles suburb, and, in 1962, received an A.A. degree from Cerritos College, in California. He attended Long Beach State on part-time status and worked as a postal carrier, but in 1964 heard from his local draft board. Three weeks before his induction notice came, he talked to an Army recruiter, who told him of something called Special Forces.

"It sounded terribly exciting." Krueger says. "This was before there was a hint of war. To get to the Special Forces, you had to go through basic training and through jump school. By April 1965, I had earned my Green Beret in Special Forces and was sent to Viet Nam."

Less than a year later, Al returned, a casualty of that war.

"In March 1966, my unit was caught in hostile fire. There were more .30-caliber machine guns than we could handle." He received enemy fire and eventually lost his left arm above the elbow.

"By the end of August 1967, I had finished a 16-month stay at Fort Sam Houston in San Antonio, Texas (recuperating). I was skinny and tired and really didn't know what I was doing, or wanted to do. I went home to California. My brother Bud, who was earlier judged unfit for service, was sport jumping at Elsinore. When he had 40 or 50 jumps, I went out to Elsinore as a spectator. That was on the day Bud had his first 60 second delay on a cheapo. In the fall of 1967, when I was watching, a Jumpmaster said, 'when are you going to start?' I hoped that everyone would say 'no' (because of my arm). I actually thought I had no chance. The Jumpmaster said, 'I think we can pull this off.'"

Krueger had made 16 static line jumps in the service, but with an artificial arm, he was back to Square One in jumping.

"I made my first sport jump October 20 in 1967. It was three years from the day I had made my first military jump.

"My first jump scared the hell out of me. It took me until February of 1968 to make my second. I asked the same question that everyone else asks, 'what the hell am I doing here?'

"But this was one big step back to reality for me—this thing (parachuting) was what I held on to. There was a place for me here . . . when I didn't have any other place . . . ."

It took 18 months for Al to make his first 100 jumps.

"I was in the sport strictly in a 'fun jump environment.' I was an 'outlaw' in the sense that I had no early interest in achievement. No license. I joined USPA only because membership was required on the DZ where I jumped. I had a Mark I PC and just generally enjoyed the party until my 900th jump or so. By that time, I had been in 60 or 80 seven-man (stars) and got my SCR on my 320th jump. We began to 'do RW ourselves.'"

Al attended the 1972 World Meet in Tahlequah, Oklahoma.

With "only" about 1,500 jumps, he was impressed with the devotion of the competitors.

"I went back to Elsinore and 12 or 15 of us began jumping as the 'Paracites' team. We were intimidated by the local skygods—either they were snobs or we were afraid to approach them. In January or February of 1973, we began to practice 10-man speed starts. The record was then in the low 40s (seconds) and Jerry Bird's All Stars was the top team.

"We thought of ourselves as a 'C' or 'D' team. We began to practice for the 1973 Nationals. We went against all the theories of practice. We jumped every weekend, four jumps or more a day. By the end of six or eight weeks of practice, our times were competitive. Then other teams saw what we were doing and began practicing. We went on to better and better practices. All of us got interested and all got our 'D' license at the same time. . . .

"We entered the 1973 Nationals. Competition times for speed stars were in the low 20s. The best teams were from California and Florida. I think there were three good California teams at that time. During the Conference meets prior to the Nationals, we had nine men and one woman on the team; during the Conference meets we entered as 'Peters Abundant and the Tunnel of Love.' PATL. In April 1973, one of the Conference manifestors used the team name all the time, over a bullhorn at a meet. All the time. He took every opportunity to use the name. I knew then that we had a poor image. That we were 'just a fun team.' I asked the team to come up with a better name than that. They chose 'Captain Hook and the Sky Pirates.' At first, I thought the name carried too much notoriety. But we worked with a majority rule and the name stayed."

Captain Hook and the Sky Pirates has become one of the best-known names in sport skydiving.

The team went to the Nationals a week early to practice. "We had three good days. The times that year (1973) were in the mid teens—15s and 16s—and the All Stars with Jerry Bird had one 14—or more. We watched what they were doing and eventually Bird's team won with 15s. A 15.7 and 15.6 and like that. . . ."

Toward the end of the Nationals, Captain Hook and the Sky Pirates were in second place behind Bird's All Stars.

Leaders in the Sport 129

Al "Captain Hook" Krueger (photo courtesy of Al Krueger)

As Al remembers it, "we got down to the end of the meet and had to have one of the fastest stars of the meet. We knew we had to have a fast one or funnel it trying. We got a 9-man (trying for a 10-man star) on the last jump and the jump killed us. The team was crushed. I was crying with the rest. But the Nationals that year taught us something. We found that RW jumpers could make the same commitment to RW and speed stars that the Style and Accuracy people were making to their own competition.

"We worked all the next year knowing that we were in second place. We were behind the All Stars. Jerry Bird had left, but it was a case of the 'A' and 'B' team. We wanted to go to the 1974 Nationals loaded for bear. We practiced out of Beeches and were making six jumps a day on the weekends, seven or eight if we had the time. We really tore ourselves up practicing. Several of us were banged up from hitting the edge of the door on the Beech exits. One of the Pirates, Sam Marshall, cracked his kneecap on the door and messed up his knee. He was carried to the plane during practices and the load was changed so no one would sit on his legs. Two or three of us had separated shoulders because of the door exits. Sam would land away from the rest of us—land in pain and away from us so we couldn't see it. He laid carpet and linoleum during the week and his legs just didn't get better."

By the end of the fifth round of competition at the 1974 Nationals, three teams were tied for the 10-man speed star event. The Wings of Orange, the All Stars, and Captain Hook and the Sky Pirates, which had always been the 'B' team in competition, were all within two seconds of each other, in total time.

"The Wings blew one of their last jumps and was between the Sky Pirates and the All Stars. On the way up for our last jump, we knew this was the Big Marble. We held hands in the middle of the plane and every 1,500 feet or so, all screamed as hard as we could to let it all out. We knew the possibility of choking because of the last year. In the freefall of the last jump, we knew we had made it. We had put together one of our best times. We took the Nationals. . . ."

The Sky Pirates had successfully beaten their "second place finish" image. Instead of slacking off, they pushed even harder, made even more commitments to their work.

Could they win, in part, because of Captain Hook?

Al Krueger packs by himself, with one hand and his hook, and he made his own commitment to his sport. Could others fail to do likewise?

As he says, in retrospect, "I don't know what differences my hook meant. We all voted for six jumps a day and when it came time for the seventh, eight of the ten voted for it and the others must have thought, 'if they can, I can,' and so we made the seventh jump of the day, or the eighth. We jumped with Sam's bad legs and with my hook and we all voted to keep on jumping."

In retrospect, the psychology of Captain Hook's hook must have played an important, if unstated role. And Captain Hook's personality. At 35, Al Krueger looks like a heavily moustached Marty Robbins. Al is congenial and modest—genuinely modest—about the Sky Pirates.

"I never thought I was the team leader. I was good at taking votes. I was riding the tide of team enthusiasm. I was never one pulling nine in tow. We all jumped together and voted together. I don't think I ever want to be the 'Larger Than Life Al Krueger. . . .' "

The Sky Pirates made their heaviest commitment yet, for the 1975 season. Prior to the 1975 Nationals, they could do no wrong. They couldn't lose a Conference Meet.

"By the time of the Nationals in Tahlequah, Oklahoma, we were ahead of everyone. We killed 'em. We won going away. We were a smooth, well-practiced team. It wasn't quite the same as 1974—there was no big gun to knock off. But in 1975, we won the right to represent the U.S. in the World Cup held in Germany. It was all a circus. We were Beech experts—experts in *that* plane—in exiting *that* plane. The Wings of Orange could change planes and jump anything well. We made 11 jumps for the World Cup—11 helicopter jumps. It was a comedy to watch. We tried 'clump exits' and that didn't work. The downdraft pushed everyone into everyone else and the thing funneled. Worse, we had practiced helicopter exits from one side of the craft and when we got to Germany for the World Cup, we discovered that the jump door was on the *other* side of the helicopter there."

By the fourth jump, the Sky Pirates were in fifth place, 14.5 seconds out of first place. "That was one whole jump-time out of first place," Captain Hook said.

"Before the fifth round, one of our Sky Pirates computed all the team averages and learned that the times we had to do to win were well within our capability. We changed everything. We went to single file exits out of the helicopters. We began to come back. The single file exits worked. Everyone had his own air and the 'clump exit' was abandoned. . . ."

As the Sky Pirates improved their times, their principal competition, the French, got worse and worse.

"By the sixth round of competition, we were in third place; on the ninth round we put together the fastest 10-man star *ever*, 12.13 seconds and were in second place, 1.5 seconds out. The French still held a thin lead.

"We had a hold for weather and finally the French went up for their last jump. We were manifesting and climbing to jump-run when they exited. All the pressure was on us and we couldn't see their jump. They worked too hard at it; their star funneled. They had a 20-second plus time. We built a respectable 14-second star. I understand that when the crowd saw the first French canopy open, and knew that the French team had blown their last star, there was applause for us, because everyone knew how hard we had tried and how far we had come from the bottom of the team rankings to challenge the lead."

When Captain Hook and his Sky Pirates landed, they had won the World Cup for the United States.

"The team went on tour—this was when everyone had 'day jobs' and supported themselves for jumping during the week—and my employer, the Crocker Bank in California, put up with a lot. I missed the tour because I had to go back and save my job. We had a meeting and I thought we would vote on how to spend the money. We received some sponsorship and the treasury had thousands and thousands of dollars in it. I thought the team would have one farewell party and break up. But one of the Pirates voted to stay together and go for the next year's competition and we took a final vote and 10 of the 12 voted to stay in—to go on.

"We had a good year in 1976. We added two new people and had a successful competition season. We did 150 practice jumps working toward the Nationals. We took first place with no hurry—again, in the ten-man speed star. The 1976 team couldn't represent the country in the World Cup because in 1976, the World Cup was held *before* the Nationals. After the 1976 Nationals, the entire team was sponsored for the Parachute Hall of Fame—and the 1976 team was specifically chosen because they didn't have a chance to go on to the World Cup competition.

"After the Nationals, in July of 1976, all 12—the Sky

The 1976 Sky Pirates (from top, clockwise) Rich Kelbaugh (alternate), Alan Babich, Steve Fielding, Bud Krueger, Mat Kelly, Jim Wallace, Ron Haun, Al "Captain Hook" Krueger, Leo Orlowski, Jeff Fisher, and Mitch Poteet. (Ray Cottingham photo)

Pirates and the alternates—wanted to go to the first Sequential Relative Work Meet, held in the northwest. But I had enough. I was burnt out. Of the 1976 team only four, myself, Al Krueger, my brother, Mitch Poteet and Leo Orlowski were left from the original Sky Pirates.

"I wanted a turn at stepping out. I wanted to retire. The team didn't believe it. We again had a meeting, right before the team was voted to the Parachute Hall of Fame and I told the team that I wanted to retire. After all, I had just completed four commitment years with the Sky Pirates. The team didn't want to believe it. They wouldn't believe it. But I did quit, after the 1976 season. . . ."

The Sky Pirates, without Al Krueger—without Captain Hook, did compete in the 1977 jump season. But there were internal squabbles and the team did not have a successful competition year. Air Freight, which was always Elsinore's 'B' team to Captain Hooks 'A' team, won the Nationals in 1977. In 1978, Air Freight won the Nationals again. Al

Krueger couldn't have been happier, for he had unselfishly passed along techniques and guidance to Air Freight from the good years that the Sky Pirates had.

In January 1979, Captain Hook had over 2,100 jumps; at 35, he holds a 'D' license, but no Gold Wings and no Diamond Wings. He has a difficult time explaining, but such awards simply don't mean much to him.

"One type of jumper enjoys the practice but hates the competition. One hates the practice and loves the competition. Thrives on competition. When you win, what do you win? A medal, a trophy? Money—that's soon spent. Or do you win recognition by your peers . . . do you gain in self growth . . . ?

"I log every jump . . . I have my 'D' license . . . and I don't take away anything from the awards (like Gold Wings) . . . but did I send in when I logged my 2,000th? No, I didn't.

"In my other life, I play banker and I don't look upon myself any differently then. I had questions I wanted to answer in skydiving and it gave me a place when I needed a place and a reason for being . . .

"Now, in 1977 and 1978, I'm back to fun jumping. . . ."

One of the most pleasing activities Captain Hook worked on was teaching a one-armed jumper from Norway how to do RW. Captain Hook got the jumper his SCR, jumping in California.

"I have sometimes been intimidated by my own history," he says, "There have been times that jumpers have, well, left me off loads because they thought I wouldn't want to jump *only* doing a three-man or *only* doing a four-man. They must have thought I wouldn't want to jump on that load. . . ."

At home, Captain Hook doesn't display much of his years with the Sky Pirates. He has six or eight framed photographs, but they are the canopy-at-sunset and ten-man-over-mountaintops photographs that any jumper could buy from a good free-fall photographer or even from a parachute supply firm. He has containers and parachute gear in the corners of his living room, but most jumpers have their gear lying around. Clearly Captain Hook enjoys the past—the achievement—the recognition by his peers—but he looks to the future of jumping, not just to the past. He jumps in 50-mans, and jumps a single-point release system, which cuts away his capewells as he pulls his reserve ripcord, a perfect system for him and he jumps because he loves the sport.

But in the future, Captain Hook will still be caught in time; there will always be those who remember the years of Captain Hook and the Sky Pirates and those who keep records in sport parachuting will not remember, or even know, what the sport gave to Captain Hook when he came home from Vietnam, a casualty of that war. Those who keep records and understand the achievements of a superb relative work team, will remember the years of speed-star achievement and the success and charisma of a modest California man known world-over as Captain Hook.

They once set 98 of the 126 world parachuting records. They give national and world-wide exhibitions. Known as "The Army's Roving Ambassadors of Goodwill," they are better known for their nickname: this is the story of...

The Golden Knights

Without a doubt, sport parachuting owes a great debt to the military: most of us learn to jump on military surplus gear; some of us still pack surplus reserves. After World War Two, after Korea, after Viet Nam, some sport parachute clubs were started or sustained by ex-military jumpers. The earliest color of gear we all knew was O.D., olive drab, sometimes now known as "sage green."

Yet military jumpers and military regulations don't seem to live well with modern sport jumping. The Golden Knights, who perform throughout the country and indeed, world-wide, have had a hard time, have endured taunts and jeers for years, achieving a place in the world of sport jumping.

But as the decade of the 70s passes, the Golden Knights may have found their own place in parachuting and, to their credit, they have done it their own way, marching to the beat of their military cadences.

According to Sgt. First Class Dave Goldie, the Golden Knights information specialist, the nucleus of the Golden Knights was established about 1959, at Fort Bragg.

"By 1959-1960," Goldie said, "a demo unit was making jumps into fairs and carnivals in North and South Carolina, from Fort Bragg. By 1961, the team was named the Army Parachute Team. In 1962, we took the name Golden Knights, a take-off on the West Point nickname, the Black Knights. We became the official Army demonstration team during this period, with installations at Fort Bragg, Fort Campbell and Fort Lewis. We are scheduled by the Department of Defense, as a unit.

"All Knights are enlisted men. This is the only service demonstration team which consists of enlisted men. All other service teams—demonstration teams such as The Thunderbirds—are officers.

"In 1959, the original team consisted of 11 men. By the end of the 1978 season, the Golden Knights had a complement of 62 men and women, counting aviators, five aircraft: two (Y)C7A Caribou and three C7As...

"Actually," Goldie said, "the Caribou is a carry-over from the Korean War. It is the only aircraft in Army service which has the capability to carry the men and equipment which the Golden Knights need. The Caribou can carry 12 jumpers, a pilot and co-pilot, a crew chief and everyone's gear. But we aren't in as good shape as the civilians are, regarding jump aircraft...." Ideally, Goldie and his colleagues would like to use the Twin Otter, but that aircraft is not Army-authorized. "Use of any other aircraft such as the Otter is a long, long, way down the road," Goldie said.

The Golden Knights are now big business. During their season, which runs from late spring through early fall, in most areas of the country, the Golden Knights will be scheduling appearances by two demonstration teams, an RW team and a style and accuracy team, which Goldie and the rest of the Knights wryly call "the loopers" (front loop, back loop...).

It wasn't long into the existence of the Knights before

Leaders in the Sport 137

Two Golden Knights check their spot (exit point) over two miles above the earth to insure a perfect, on "target", landing. (U.S. Army photo by SFC Joe Sumakeris)

their schedule and determination that "the show must go on," brought tragedy to the team.

On March 8, 1973, a demonstration team departed Fort Bragg for a scheduled tour in Kansas. Shortly after take-off, the C-47 (which was then used by the team) encountered, in Goldie's words, "one of the worst electrical storms ever seen in North Carolina." The C-47 literally broke up in flight. All the Knights aboard were killed when the debris hit the ground. Lost in that incident were: SFC Francis P. Welch, team leader; Sp5 Edward M. Parrish, Team Photographer; Pfc. Paul D. Albritton; Ssg. Joseph Babbarick; Sgt. Michael G. Buckley; Ssg. Cecil E. Davis; Ssg. Raymond C. Kinser; Ssg.

Joseph B. Pelter; Ssg. James F. Rice; Ssg. Michael D. Walsey; Ssg. Robert T. Wolfe; CW3 Richard A. Del Conte, Pilot; CW2 Rodney H. Pease, Co-pilot; and Ssg. Bartley L. Bullington, Crew Chief.

Parachutist magazine later reported:

> On Thursday morning, March 8, 1973, sport parachuting suffered a tragic loss when the U.S. Army Parachute Team's C-47 broke up in flight from causes as yet undetermined, carrying to their deaths all 14 team members on board. They were enroute from Simmons Army Air Force Base at Fort Bragg, North Carolina to Overland Park, Kansas, to begin a 15-day recruiting tour in support of Army recruiting efforts.
>
> Conditions were IFR, with low ceiling and turbulence reported. The aircraft was routed by Air Traffic Control into the sector operated by the Raleigh-Durham approach control facility. Communications with the plane were normal, and a final radio message directed the plane to 'report 4,000.' The aircraft never reached that altitude but was seen by the radar operator to do a sudden 180-degree course reversal and then disappear from the screen.
>
> Observers believe that the aircraft suffered structural failure in flight, losing first a wing and then other components. Wreckage of the plane was spread over a mile of countryside near Silk Hope, North Carolina. There were no survivors.
>
> The Army Parachute Team announced immediately that the schedule of Team activities would continue and that a new group would be formed to carry on the duties and responsibilities of the men who died.

Parachutist magazine also later succinctly editorialized "...they served well our country and our sport."

According to Goldie, "We then went into the business of fulfilling our commitments . . ." The Knights recruit new members for the various squads later in the year—during December. Those who don't make the Knights are told to return to their original units and try the Knights again the next year. The Knights had only to screen the applicants who had failed the previous December's try-outs, to cull new replacements for the lost men.

(In 1970, prior to the loss of the Knights in the C-47 crash, one Golden Knight died during a demonstration jump. Staff Sergeant Arnoldo A. Arrellano died in Corpus Christi, Texas, June 20; he deployed his main, which entangled around a smoke bracket on his foot. The entanglement developed into a horseshoe malfunction which was never cut away. As a result of Sgt. Arrellano's death, the Army Parachute Team redesigned the smoke bracket and added quick-release bindings to avoid such a problem in the future.)

The Golden Knights' entry into serious relative work competition was seriously handicapped by the 1973 crash.

"The C-47 crash cost us our first effort at RW," Goldie said, "that put us about three years behind. In late '73, we entered our first trial ten-man team. We subsequently determined to stay out of RW until we had the manpower to do it right . . ."

By the middle 1970s the style and accuracy teams were making names for themselves. There have been eight or nine national champions from the Golden Knights; from 1962-1973, the Knights produced four world champions and once set 98 of the 126 world parachuting records. Needless to say, the Golden Knights are always keenly interested in beating the Russian Parachuting teams. Once, during the late 1970s Cheryl Stearns, the only woman then serving on the Golden Knights, beat *everyone* on the Russian men's team.

While none of the Golden Knights are officers, all pay particular attention to the USPA-sanctioned awards and ratings. "All the Knights are USPA 'D' (license holders)," Goldie says, "many of the Knights have the Gold Wings for their thousandth jump and several have made 4,000 skydives . . ."

Gear for the Golden Knights varies from year to year, depending on availability of components and depending on the speciality of each Knight.

"During the 1978 season, the style and accuracy people—the "loopers"—wore chest reserves, one-pin mains and capewells. The RW people jumped super light gear, one-pin releases and Booth three-ring circuses. The demo squads wore tandems, jumped Clouds and used capewells . . ."

Just like other Army units, the Golden Knights advertise for bids on supplies. Would the Knights buy gear cheaper than civilian units? "Usually not," Goldie says, "actually there aren't that many suppliers interested in bidding on our gear. We have to actually buy higher than civilians do. We have had to beg to get some gear. For several years we couldn't get the Wonderhog in army green. Now it is made for us (in green) and sold internationally, too, for other military units. Although we end up paying more for gear, we serve a good function for suppliers in other ways—we test new innovations, new gear, new state-of-the-art. If something works, the manufacturer will offer it—if we discover some malfunction, that piece of equipment will never get to the jumping public...."

In the immediate past—during the 1976, 1977 and 1978 seasons, the demo units jumped StratoClouds, Parafoils, Strato Flyers and Viking 'chutes. Because most of the demonstration jumpers must repack on concrete, airport rampways or other similar areas, their gear takes a beating. The demo jumpers go through three complete sets of gear each season, with harness and containers the first to wear out. The Golden Knights, as part of their logistics and supply arm, employ five Master riggers, and ten Senior riggers. All their gear is TSO'ed.

Like the Ringling Brothers Circus, which has two traveling companies, the Golden Knights have the "Gold" and "Black" demonstration teams. The full complement for the Knights is 44 jumpers and 18 supply, logistics and support personnel. The operation costs $245,000 each year, but that is a "deceptive figure," according to Goldie, as each public appearance away from Fort Bragg must be sponsored by a civilian group, which must pay $33 per day per man, which is forwarded to the U.S. Department of the Treasury. "It's kind of a 'You buy, We Fly' operation," Goldie says.

"Since 1959, the Golden Knights have made 190,000 jumps," Goldie says, "we have had one fatality and two other Knights died in sport jumping entirely unrelated to Knight activity. They died during off-hours jumping at a civilian sport parachute club in the Fort Bragg area."

One Golden Knight who narrowly missed death was Sgt. Roger Reynolds. On April 24, 1974, the demo team was appearing at a regional celebration, the Dogwood Festival at Charlottesville, Virginia. Sgt. Reynolds' specialty was the cutaway, a deliberate breakaway from a parachute designed to malfunction. Sgt. Reynolds had done the cutaway successfully a dozen times previously and had practiced the cutaway procedure about 50 times.

The cutaway rig has not one, but two sets of capewells on the shoulders of the jumper. The top set has to be activated to chop the deliberately malfunctioning parachute.

Four-man non-contact RW jumping, with smoke brackets. The Golden Knights excel in this kind of close-work demonstration jumping. (photo courtesy of The Golden Knights)

The second, or bottom set would be used in case the second main failed to deploy. At that time, if needed, the second set could be used to cut away the second main and he could come down on his reserve.

That day, the sky was full of scud from rains. Reynolds jumped at 2,000 feet, lower than usual for the cutaway.

In free-fall, he opened the first chute, which would deliberately malfunction. But he activated *one* of the top set of capewells, and one of the *lower* set. A streamer resulted.

Goldie: "It simply wasn't Sgt. Reynolds' time to die. Because of the stress on the one capewell which Reynolds didn't cut away, he fell at an angle and the capewell locked closed. He fought with the capewell all the way down. If he had looked down, he might have tensed for the ground contact and been killed. But he was looking up at the risers all the time, and when he hit, he hit almost sideways..."

It wasn't his time to die...

"He landed in a civilian's front yard near the festival. In the back yard, at the same time, was the homeowner, a doctor—a surgeon—giving a barbeque for six or seven of his friends, all surgeons.

"In less than a half a minute, Sgt. Reynolds had the best medical help he could have possibly received in the area...."

Later, in the September, 1978 issue of *The Saturday Evening Post*, in an article about the incident, "I Thought I Was Going To Die," writer Tom Keating estimated that Sgt. Reynolds hit the ground at 80 miles per hour.

Reynolds sustained a broken left arm, broken left leg, cracked pelvis, and injuries to his shoulder, ribs, hip, ankle and heels, in addition to internal injuries.

Fourteen months after the accident, Reynolds removed his last cast.

It wasn't his time..."

Reynolds served out his tour with The Golden Knights and made further skydives because he wanted to "quit the sport on my terms...."

Did the Golden Knights learn anything from the Reynolds incident? "Yes," Goldie says, "we redesigned the cutaway system so that the second set of capewells doesn't appear until the jumper has cut away the first chute. A lot of different things happened in the Reynolds' jump. Many of the causes could have been prevented. We know how to redesign our gear...."

Many past or present members of the Golden Knights are international names in parachuting and skydiving: 1975 national champion Ron Walker; '75 National Style champion Jack Brake; two-time Pan-Am Champion and '73 National Champion Chuck Collingwood; '71 National Accuracy Champion Don Strickland; '76 U.S. Team members Bill Knight and Dennis Sattler; Major Chuck Whittle; '73 National Collegiate Champion Bill Wenger; Cheryl Stearns, who beat the Russian men's team...and many others....

What of the Golden Knights' RW chances?

According to Sgt. First Class Fred O'Donnell, the RW team leader, "The Knights trained five weeks for the first RW competition we ever entered...in my way of thinking it was the wrong meet—the Z-Hills (Zephyr Hills, Florida) 1976 Turkey meet. We didn't have a hell of a lot of know-how. We got some help from Scratch Garrison and Roger Hull, who taught

The moment of truth: as the ground rushes up at over 120 MPH, this Golden Knight pulls his ripcord 2,000 feet above the ground. (U.S. Army photo by SFC Joe Sumakeris)

us the basics for two weeks. We ended up fourth in the eight-man competition. The Z-Hills people looked at us with considerable skepticism. No one thought we could do serious RW or sequential RW *as a military unit*. The Z-Hills people thought that the chemistry of a good RW team wouldn't be possible for the Knights. But I had been in jumping on and off since 1960 and all the really good RW teams I have ever seen had their own discipline. I didn't think that military discipline was necessarily wrong for RW team-efforts. It (military discipline) is not counter-productive for RW work. But the Z-Hills people were more shocked than we were. For a lot of people, our entry was a rude awakening. I know we impressed some. The majority? . . . no. Pat Works wrote that we were 'reeking with respectability.' We met tolerance, not acceptance.

"I had told the Commander of the Knights that, if the Knights were interested in supporting our RW efforts, we could give them a national championship team within 18-24 months. The Commander *did* support us—and we had our championship team in 15 months—in July, 1978."

O'Donnell, who holds "D" 3693, has made 2,300 jumps, has his SCR, SCS, Night SCR, Women's SCR and his 12-hour Free Fall pin.

"I think 1978 was our breakthrough year," he says, of the Knights RW efforts, "in March of '78, we took the Military National Championships; in May, we won the USPA Mideast Conference Championships; in June, the USPA Southeast Conference Championships; in July, we became National Champions; and in September, we became the World Champions in France."

The November, 1978 issue of *Parachutist* said:

> In a solid performance which included one 7-point round, the United States captured the top spot in the 8-man sequential event of the 4th World Cup of Relative Work held at Mourmelon-le-Grande, France, September 21-October 1.
>
> Representing the United States and USPA were the U.S. Army Parachute Team, the 'Golden Knights', who were the winners at the 1978 National Championships. The Knights headed a field of 10 teams with a 22 point effort, outdistancing the Icarus team of France and the Springboks of South Africa by 2 and 9 points, respectively.
>
> The 4-man event, called after two rounds due to inclement weather, was won by South Africa's Springbok team, who scored 12 points in the abbreviated competition. The U.S. placed second with a score of 11 points, tied with another team from South Africa and one from France for the runner-up spot.
>
> The 8-man team amassed an impressive 7 points on their third jump, ending the round with facing diamonds. With the formation

completed, the diamonds separated and tracked in opposite directions until pull time. This maneuver startled ground observers and created a 'fabulous psychological effect' on the other teams, according to Captain Marty Jeppesen, head of the U.S. delegation.

Participating in the 8-man competition were Knights Michael Bachman, Matt McManus, Fred O'Donnell, Reed Robbins, Stephen Salisbury, Michael Sweeney, Patrick Van Bibber, Craig Van Camp and Bill Wenger.

"I think that '79 and '80 will be tough years for us," O'Donnell said, "everyone is always gunning for Number One. We'll have to put in much more effort. We expend ninety percent of our effort on the 8-man work, rather than the four-man or the ten-man . . . we are in RW to stay now . . . and the Knights are attracting people who would have never considered joining the Army at all . . . .

"If I would state one disappointment, I'd have to say that we were never able to meet the '77 National winners, the Mirror Image team from California. That was the team that had given birth to the event—8-man RW. Mirror Image had B. J. Worth, Curt Curtis and Roger Hull . . . some of the Mirror Image bunch did later compete with us on an individual basis . . . but we never did meet the team that began it all. . . ."

There is little doubt that the Golden Knights are military first and sky divers and competitors second. All the Golden Knights have checking accounts with the Knights crest on their personal checks. If a Knight bounces a check in the Fort Bragg area, he will lose his job. O'Donnell explained it in a chauvanistic way: "If a guy is married and his wife screws up his checking account, he can lose his job with the Knights . . . ."

The Knights are also instructed to leave a cocktail party immediately if any civilian lights up a joint of marijuana. "If any Knight would stay, that would mean that the Knights condone the use of marijuana," Sgt. Goldie explains. "No Knights smoke dope . . . Knights never get drunk . . . we give prospective members every chance during their six-week recruitment period. For every jump any of the Golden Knights make on recruiting missions or demonstrations anywhere, each Knight may attend five or six cocktail parties as part of their public relations effort. We do not tolerate Knights who can't hold their composure."

The Golden Knights may be the most conservative sky divers in the country. "Sure," Sgt. Goldie says "We probably *are* the most conservative sky divers in the nation. We never endanger the crowds. Period. We are the only F.A.A. recognized demo team in the country. But we never ask for a waiver of F.A.A. regs. We do it all within the F.A.A. guidelines. We'll probably be the last team in the country to switch to square reserves. When you join the Golden Knights, you make a pact with the Devil—you no longer have a personal life and everything you do—you do for the Golden Knights. We have to meet every day with many, many civic leaders. Mayors, city councilmen and the like . . . and the last real contact they had with the Army was probably during the Korean War. We have to convince them the Army is not like the 'M.A.S.H.' We constantly sell the Army. We have to re-educate everyone we meet. Most of the Knights *enjoy* selling the Army. They are dedicated to recruiting . . . ."

Within the scope of sport skydiving, the Golden Knights are determined to do it *their* way. The Army way.

He has jumped from heights sky divers have only dreamed about. His has been the highest high. This is . . .

Col. Joe Kittinger's Story

His parachute logbook appears only mediocre; 101 jumps. Many sky divers have hundreds, even thousands more. Many make one hundred jumps in a few weeks. Some, setting sport records, make a hundred jumps in a few hours. But Joe Kittinger's jumps are perhaps the best, most unusual and most facinating one-hundred-and-one jumps ever made.

And because he is a modest man, when asked for a signature

he once wrote "To . . . a fellow jumper—from a novice. Joe Kittinger."

Yet thousands of pilots owe their lives to experiments he made, successful jumps he made, successful devices he tested.

Joe Kittinger, the *novice*. With only a P.C.A. (Parachute Club of America, forerunner to the United States Parachute Association) class "B" license.

Joe Kittinger was born in Florida and grew up in the swamps of central Florida. Like Charles Lindbergh, who went on to flying after outgrowing motorcycles, Joe Kittinger (pronounced like *fitting-her*) graduated to airplanes from racing boats in the lakes and rivers of his home. He remembers learning a healthy respect for the snarling, fragile craft; he learned speed, movement, safety, motivation, grace and courage. He was barely in high school.

In 1949, he joined the Air Force as an aviation cadet. After receiving his wings in 1950 at the Las Vegas Air Force Base, Nevada, he served with the 86th Fighter Bomber Wing in Germany, for three years. He returned to the United States in 1953 and was assigned to the Fighter Test Section at Holloman Air Force Base, New Mexico.

On dreary duty, flying paratroops to El Centro, California, Kittinger was challenged to "make a jump."

"I volunteered, 'cause I was 'just a mortal,' " he laughs. "There was tremendous camaraderie. I remember that—and the gear. I jumped a 28-foot flat circular canopy. A T-7. There was a tremendous opening shock . . ."

Kittinger stayed with it. Jumping when and where he could, he eventually ended his career with 60 civilian jumps. His others were all military.

He served at Holloman until 1958, when his next duty assignment took him to the Aerospace Medical Laboratory in Dayton, Ohio, where he served as Project Engineer and Test Director until 1963. It was during this phase of Col. Kittinger's career that he achieved the highest high.

On November 16, 1959, Col. Kittinger stepped out of a balloon at 76,400 feet to test high altitude survival equipment.

As he says, "Our purpose in the high altitude tests was always to provide the pilot with the proper physiological environment to take care of him 'in spite of himself.' Don't forget that for many pilots, their first parachute jump comes without training. Certainly without skydiving experience. We needed to devise an escape system for very high altitudes which would support the pilot. Capsules for every pilot in every type of aircraft are too expensive and too cumbersome. There is too much trade-off between weight and protection. We need to devise a pressure suit and stabilization parachutes. At the time we knew we needed this material. This testing. So we did it. There were a lot of people telling us not to (make these high jumps). We couldn't build an escape system for all regimes of flight, but we did need a reliable pressure suit and parachute system which would keep the pilot safe until he could get down to a survival atmosphere . . . ."

Because he has been there and back down, Kittinger instinctively stresses the *hostile environment* of space. For at 76,000 feet and later, at 102,000 feet, he was above 98 percent of the earth's atmosphere and with sub-zero temperatures. *A hostile arena.* His phrases are sometimes different but never vague. In fact, Col. Kittinger very nearly died there, on the edge of space, with equipment tested just before his jump, much less perfected.

At 76,000 feet, Col. Kittinger, wearing a full body pressure suit like our later astronauts, stepped out of a special balloon. He had a modified static line system, the Beaupre MultiStage Parachute. The Beaupre parachute was designed specifically for stabilization, and to take the pilot down into safer, breatheable air, without endangering his life needlessly by prolonged exposure to the dangers of high altitudes. To open a parachute canopy at 76,000 feet would be sheerest folly; in the high thin air of that altitude, the pilot's life would be threatened several ways; the parachute, built for 'normal' opening shocks of less than 150 m.p.h. would probably rip to shreds if the pilot opened in thin air of high altitudes. In fact, at 76,000 feet, the free-fall pilot or sky diver would build up speeds in excess of 600 m.p.h.

If his parachute survived opening at those speeds, the pilot would still be exposed to sub-zero temperatures which would kill; he would also be exposed, without adequate pressure suits, to an atmosphere so thin the air would be incapable of sustaining life. Thus Kittinger and his team had these three problems to solve simultaneously: to control descent to allow a parachute to open successfully; to control the environment to keep the pilot warm at the edges of space; and to keep him surrounded with a life-support suit which would feed him breathable oxygen until he got to lower altitudes and could open his faceplate.

The Beaupre MultiStage Parachute, once activated, would begin a timer which would, in turn, fire a six-foot drag chute, to keep the falling pilot stable in free-fall. Eventually a barometer, sensing altitude and speed, would fire automatically and open the main chute.

Now, most major parachute centers offer their novice jumpers the use of a Sentinel, an automatic barometric-and-speed computer which will open the novice jumper's reserve if there is no open canopy over the jumper's head as he or she passes through the last 1,000 feet. In 1959, with Col. Kittinger at 76,000 feet, choices of automatic openers, parachute deployment systems and jumpsuit designs were critical.

In the following passage from his book, *The Long, Lonely Leap*, Col. Kittinger tells how it feels to disconnect the life-support system from his balloon gondola and step into a free-fall from 76,000 feet....

> I stand in the gondola .... Now that the radios are disconnected, I am cut off from the world 76,000 feet below. The lack of sound is amost a crash of silence. Something penetrates the emptiness, a wheezing that hisses directly in my ears. It is the sound of my own breathing in the pressure helmet.
>
> I shuffle clumsily to the narrow opening , and stop. I am incredibly awkward. Now I bend my trunk forward just slightly to place my arms outside the thin aluminum wall of the gondola, in space.
>
> I grasp the lanyard which is attached to the two timers of the parachute.
>
> This is my final connection to the gondola, the last of the umbilical cords to be severed. With my right hand—clumsily, because of the restricting confines of the pressure suit—I make a hard, outward, pulling motion. I stare at the lanyard in disbelief— the arming times fail to pull free!
>
> Quickly I pull again, as hard as I can. A third time—and finally the timer knobs pull free. With a short, disgusted motion I fling them away from me. I reach back for my final task aboard the

gondola, and punch the button that starts all the data cameras running.

I hesitate for a moment, and grant myself that time to look down at the earth, 76,000 feet below me . . . and take a small, ludicrous short hop.

I fall away from the balloon, face down and my arms out, staring at the earth. I am unaware that I hold my breath. There is no sound. Not a whisper of wind. No vibration.

Nothing.

Nothing?

No sensation . . . absolutely no sensation at all. I cannot be falling! This cannot be real . . . . My thoughts whirl crazily. Something fantastic, impossible, is happening to me. A roaring that is without sound thunders in my brain.

I do not move . . . *I'm not falling!*

Never have I known or even remotely dreamed of anything like this. I stare, hard. I think my eyes are bulging in their sockets. This world is insane.

There is only . . . nothing. The flatness is far below, frozen in time and space. My brain spins . . . time itself has ground to a halt.

That earth down there, so far below . . . I want desperately, with all my heart and soul, *to fall.*

What is happening to me?

It is as though God looked down and for some reason inexplicable to me, far beyond any comprehension I might ever receive, He reached out and stopped the world and time and space and everything in it from moving.

There is no time. Never before, never again will I know the freezing numbness of unreality that steals through my mind and my body. Seconds . . . hours . . . no time.

Then comes the first intrusion into the void. A vibration, a tiny tremor that starts at my back. I hear the sound, feel the vibration through my body. What is . . . .

The timer for the stabilization chute! But . . . how long has it been since I stepped out of the gondola? It cannot be time yet.

I take a grip on my chaotic thoughts. The reality of the moment is the vibration of the timer. Instinctively, I tense for the parachute to pull free, for the canopy to deploy to its diameter of six feet; I wait for the slight tug.

Nothing happens.

I wait . . . Again an *absence* of anything happening. The seconds stretch on, drag out.

The terrifying thought flashes through my mind that the chute has fouled, that it has snarled around my body.

A horrible mental picture, brilliant and garish and frightening—my body spinning helplessly toward the earth, just as I have seen the dummies in the early tests tumbling, snarled in their parachutes, whirling crazily all the way down to earth.

I become frantic. Yet there remains some semblance of control, a reserve ability to *think*. I pull in my arms and run my gloved hands down my legs. As though watching from a distance, I see my hands move with amazing precision down my legs, searching for the fouled parachute. But I am only a blind man groping in his eternal darkness.

My hands find . . . nothing.

I begin to roll over in the accelerating plunge to earth. I am . . . where? . . . I am on my back. My face is up; I am falling on my back, head down.

I am unaware at this moment that, in these agonizing seconds since leaving the gondola, 16,000 feet have vanished. At 60,000 feet my body reaches its terminal velocity, plunging through the air at 423 miles per hour. The temperature of the air about me is 104 degrees below zero. But I know none of these things at this time.

Slowly, my body begins to turn to the left. Instantly, I recognize the motion; I have made many free-falls, of up to sixty seconds duration. My reaction is instinctive—immediately I drop my left arm.

The spin ends at once.

Then there is a new movement. My body begins a turn to the right, I drop my right leg, lower my right arm. Again the spinning stops even as it begins.

The thought comes to me that I can, perhaps, employ this technique all the way down into denser atmosphere. There has been only that one burst of panic. I still know fear; fear that is very much with me but not enough to prevent my thinking trying to rationalize, doing what I can to overcome . . . whatever it is. It must be the parachute, snarled around my body, *somewhere*.

Perhaps there is the chance now that I may be able to fall semi-stabilized into the denser air, to continue to control my body movements. Yes, with care, with constant attention to what happens, I can fall safely to lower attitude. . . .

No sooner do I find comfort in this thought than a tremendous hand explodes out of nowhere and slaps my body to the left, a stunning push that I cannot believe. In this instant my body spins crazily.

Again my movements are instinctive, I shoot out my left leg and arm to stop the spin. It has no effect.

I remember everything I know of the dreaded spin; now I follow my own lessons, heed my own warnings, I pull in my arms and legs, pull into a ball, knees up, arms close. My rate of spin seems almost to explode.

Now! I fling out my arms. I am a body, jerking spasmodically, deliberately, into the spread-eagle position.

No good! The spin comes!

Now comes the deadliest sound of all, the whisper of danger rushing after me.

Swish!

Swish!

Swish!

Faster and faster, still accelerating, faster and faster! I sink into helplessness. I realize fully that as my body increases its speed in the spin I am hurtling into a situation that may rob me of all conscious volition to help myself.

I can feel it, a sickening sensation washing over me; invisible forces whirl my body around. Faster . . . .

I want the spinning to stop; I want nothing so desperately in all my life.

I pray . . . I feel that I will die.

On my left arm is the altimeter, I want to look at the dial: I *must* look at the dial to see if I am low enough to pull the ripcord of the reserve parachute to stop the spinning. I try to pull in my left arm . . . .

I cannot move! I cannot move my arms or my legs. I am immobile, as if the centrifugal force whirling me around had jabbed me helplessly onto some enormous stakes thrust through my body and each of my limbs.

I cannot hold down the panic. It wells up, bubbling and black and red. I know what is happening, I am sick with fear; I can do nothing.

I am losing peripheral vision.

And then, praying as hard as I can, praying for my life to be spared . . . I see the dark curtains closing.

Blackness crashes down on me.

Again there is no time.

I open my eyes. My mind wanders. What . . .? There has been blackness—how can I see? Am I alive?

Then, slowly, there comes the glorious wonder of the sight before my eyes. There, above me, the marvelous shape of the canopy, the red and white panels straining beautifully into the air, holding me, lowering me in the harness safely toward the earth. I want to shout with the joy and wonder of it!

I will not know for some time yet what has happened—Francis Beaupre has saved my life. The line between the small pilot chute and the main canopy of the reserve parachute is made to withstand a pull of more than 1,500 pounds. Beaupre had calculated, however, that if ever I needed the reserve parachute, I might be unconscious. He proceeded in his genius to extrapolate a situation in which I might be spinning, and the aneroid would automatically deploy the parachute. Were this to happen, he reasoned, then the pilot chute would emerge, only to entangle in the main canopy of the chute that must be snarled. This man saw all this in my mind, and replaced the strong nylon with a line of only one-tenth its strength.

Because he did so, I lived. Later, I would study the film from the camera in my instrument kit. I would see the canopy tangled above me. The tremendous force of the spin whirled the pilot chute around; but, as Beaupre planned, the weaker nylon line snapped. This freed the reserve chute main canopy. It caught the air, blossomed outward and filled, eleven seconds after opening. I know nothing of this as I drift toward the earth. I know only that I am impossibly, wonderfully *alive*. The sound of the helicopter's blades reaches my ears.

Minutes later, I drop into the white gypsum sands of the desert, roll over on my back. I do not move.

The main parachute is wrapped around my neck.

I lie there on the sands as the men from the helicopter rush toward me. Gratitude spills in a torrent into me.

I whisper, *"Thank you, God...."*

I cannot forget, then or later, or now, those men, the men of my team who tried to foresee every eventuality ... and who gave me back my life.

Something did go terribly, horribly wrong. But what? Films taken from the bottom of the balloon gondola and later retrieved revealed the problem. Kittinger activated his parachute system, but activated it too soon. He should have waited at least 16 seconds, to build up air speed, to give the pilot chute a chance to clear his back and deploy cleanly. But he activated the parachute deployment system at the edge of the gondola and then disconnected other systems. His parachute began deployment sequences less than three seconds after he cleared the bottom of the gondola.

Without sufficient air speed to reach terminal, the pilot chute bounced helplessly on his shoulders, an awesome feeling as many sky divers can testify, and then knotted around his neck. Photos taken by the U. S. Air Force later showed Kittinger on the ground, groggy, with the bridle line *still around his neck.*

Abashed that he had nearly died because of improper techniques at the edge of space—at the edge of the gondola—Kittinger demanded that he retake the 76,000 jump. Less than a month later, he did remake that jump. The timer fired perfectly, he fell until he reached 18,000 feet, the canopy blossomed as it should and the test was a success.

Yet the tests were not complete. Kittinger and his team—project Excelsior—always believed that there was an invisible barrier at the 100,000 level, like the sound barrier. Kittinger later explained, "We thought that from 76,000 feet, if any part of the pressure suit malfunctioned, the pilot *might* have a chance to survive. That he could fall into a safe environment before the malfunction produced a fatality. But over 100,000 feet, any error or malfunction would be critical. The height would preclude any chance of a safe return to a safe arena."

Thus the barrier. A barrier that Kittinger challenged, for the sake of all pilots who might have to eject at altitude. In his book, *The Long, Lonely Leap*, Kittinger recounts his ascent in the balloon and jump, made August 16, 1960, from 102,800 feet. As he fell, he spoke into a helmet microphone, which was taped, thus he could relive his jump later.

> My words drifted away . . . .
>
> I had much to do in the eleven minutes I would remain at float altitude, a brief visit within the shoreline of the alien world I had breached. During these minutes that I drifted along the edge of space, a sensation of awe grew within me. The realization of where I stood crashed home with a jubilant roar in my mind.
>
> I felt a surging mixture of emotion. The marvelous sense of accomplishment, of exhultation, hammered down the fear generated by my presence in the bitterly hostile environment about me. Now not even that fear could diminish the wonder I knew and gratefully savored.
>
> I looked at space . . . the first man ever to see through only a thin faceplate the environment we were sworn to storm, to use one day as we now indifferently used the lower atmosphere.

The few men who had reached here before me suffered a vision clouded by their combinations of faceplates, double-walled windows, aircraft canopies, and other obstructions.

I went to work . . . and immediately found the effort sucking energy from my body. For hours I had worn 150 pounds of equipment, and then absorbed the requirements of 90 minutes of balloon ascent with its pressure suit constriction and pressure breathing. The effect of my swollen right hand, the emotional storms through which I'd passed, all these had sapped my energy. Every move I made in the gondola demanded a concentrated effort.

Despite my desire to continue my study of space unhindered, the blinding glare of direct solar radiation forced me to shade the sunlight with my left hand. My eyes quickly burned and smarted if I made the mistake of looking directly, even through the visor, at that fearsome orb in the heavens, free to my sight of cloying dust, water vapor, smoke, and the denser air of the surface.

The gondola turned slowly; each time the sun burst through the open hatchway it felt like exactly what it was—a strong blast of heat. During these seconds, one side of me baked in the glare; the other, in shadow, sent off from my flying suit a steamlike vapor of heat.

The circulation in my hand had come almost to a halt. The hand was a leaden, cold thing, its only sensation an uncomfortable pain I could not indefinitely ignore.

But it was easy at moments to forget the pain . . . for the balloon drifted within a gentler stream of wind, moving at a ground speed of 30 miles per hour, and so placid was this drifting that I seemed almost to be suspened between deep space and a bottomless ocean beneath the gondola. There was not the slightest vertical motion, not even a whisper of a rise or descent. The great beautiful balloon had achieved its rest in the sky.

It was time to prepare for the jump . . . I called ground control for their estimate. Marv came back almost immediately "Three minutes till jump, Joe."

The countdown reached to minus 90 seconds. It was time to tell the doctor about my hand. "For your information, Marv, my right hand is not pressurized." Marv must have had a hard time to keep from exploding at me; his questions came in machine-gun fashion through the earphones. (He told me later he had a short statement all prepared for this moment, a parting gesture, but that my report about the glove so shocked him he forgot the whole thing.) But above all, he wanted me to get out of that gondola, and to get out immediately.

"Okay. No sweat. No sweat," I called back. Minus 70 seconds . . .

I jettisoned the trailing antenna. Seventy seconds left up there, absolutely cut off from the world. Seventy seconds: these were mine. One by one I cut the umbilical cords connecting me to the gondola, transferring responsibility for my life through pressure and oxygen to the seat kit.

I stood up and shuffled clumsily to the open hatchway of the gondola, my feet just over the edge.

The medical records show that my pulse raced to 136 per minute. They reveal that at X minus 20 seconds I took a deep breath, then exhaled quickly. A breath, a short exhalation, another breath—and I would hold this last breath for the next 18 seconds....

I stood in the open door of the gondola... perhaps for 45 seconds. The gondola turned very slowly. For those seconds I did not move.

Then I looked up at the sky, as high as I could look. I had a fleeting thought that there was almost a challenge flung out; a whisper in my own mind. *"I've beaten you so far...."* Words only for myself.

Then Excelsior I flashed through my mind, and this was replaced almost immediately by the far more pleasant thoughts of Excelsior II.

I looked down at the clouds; turned, and depressed the button to start all the cameras whirring... shutter and motors, gears grinding, eleven cameras going off with a clanking and clashing of gears.

Now I grasped the lanyard with my right hand... it was useless. My hand was swollen, painful, cold; I could not pull the lanyard. I let it go; my own weight as I fell would pull out the timer knob for the stabilization parachute.

I placed my hands on the edge of the gondola; in these last fleeting moments, all the grandeur and beauty of the fantastic world I was about to leave came home to me again.

One day, not too distant in the future, this height might—will—become familiar to men. They will regard this hostile arena in much the same way as our airmen today regard the atmosphere in which they fly regularly.

Some day; but not now.

Now—home lay straight down. To reach there safely was a task beyond my control.

Somebody else must help me.

I looked up, and the words rang sharp and clear as I said: *"Lord, take care of me now..."*

I stepped out—102,800 feet above the earth.

For the third time in my life I know the fantasy of being

suspended in space, my body defying the law of gravity. No wind hisses in my ears or billows my clothing. There is no sound, no movement . . .

Only for the briefest of moments. The instant I leave the balloon I start to kick my arms and legs. This time *I* am going to control everything that happens to me!

As I fall away from the gondola, I kick my arms and legs vigorously to begin a roll to the left. I have absolute control of my body, and my rapid leg and arm movements twist my body in the fall so that I roll around to a position on my back. It seems that I do not fall, but simply twist my body position around. And then, exhulting in this precise control, I leave the edge of space, falling as I wish on my back so I may look up . . . .

There, not over a hundred feet away, looms a tremendous globe of incandescent white light. It is fully two hundred feet in diameter, and glows a brilliant and rich white . . . the great balloon against a backdrop of the absolute black of space.

I hold my breath. There is no noise, no sound, no sensation of acceleration or falling; that same nothingness of Excelsior I. But that jump is now behind me, a matter of experience; anticipating the sensation, I am free of alarm, free to look.

The fantastic sight before my eyes is stunning to behold. I am suspended in space. Above me the brilliant globe of the balloon shoots away, explodes *upward* from the earth with unbelievable speed, shrinking rapidly in size. With impossibly swift acceleration the shining globe rockets away from the earth . . . if I did not know that the balloon still floated serenely, I would swear that I was not moving. But of course, I am accelerating rapidly toward the earth.

I look for the stars . . . dropping on my back I am desperate to see the celestial display as no man has ever seen it, my eyes separated from space only by the thin faceplate. I have an opportunity no man has ever known and that few will ever know; falling so high above the earth, and free to gaze upon space itself.

Bitter disappointment stabs at me . . . for I cannot see the stars; this golden, glittering opportunity, lost forever!

It is a dream I have cherished for many years, that grew with the recent months to a fierce hope. But I am to be denied the heavens . . . I am light-blinded. I see only the shrinking white dot of the balloon against an impenetrable velvet-blackness.

I seem not to make the move consciously, but with my left hand I now grasp the ripcord. Perhaps it will be necessary to open the stabilization chute by manual pull; I do not know, but I am prepared to yank the D-ring.

I wrench my eyes from the blackness above me and stare at the second-hand of the timer strapped to my wrist. Each second ticks away in ponderous slow-motion . . . then—there it is! Exactly 16 seconds after stepping out from the gondola, I feel the trembling vibration of the timer. At once I am conscious of the minor jolt as the timer yanks the cable to release the pins of the pack strapped to my body.

There is no opening shock . . . nothing at all! I do not change position after the timer fires; the thought flashes to me that I must use the manual override.

There is no need to do so. Suddenly I realize I am falling with my feet to earth. There has been no opening shock whatsoever! Only a gradual, unnoticeable change from unstabilized free-fall to attainment of our goal—I am stabilized as I plunge toward the earth.

[I must for a moment interrupt my narrative. Fortunately, all my equipment during the Excelsior III descent functioned perfectly. As I fell toward the earth, still accelerating, I described my reactions—and the tape recorder within the instrument kit strapped to me faithfully captured every word. Doctors A. Marko and George Potor of the Aerospace Medical Laboratories' Bioelectronics Section overcame the problems of this tape equipment in the previous jumps, thus assuring a spoken record that—if I may be guilty of understatement—has since enabled me to relive with a profound sense of strangeness and shock my jump from 102,800 feet down to the earth.

Because there is no more dramatic—and certainly no more honest record of the jump, than this tape, I have written down here the exact words I spoke. They are capitalized on the succeeding pages. With them I have taken the liberty of enlarging upon my brief statements, perhaps to impart to them a greater meaning. I wish to assure the reader that each time I listened to this recording I felt all the emotions I knew then, and relived in my mind every second of that fall. The altimeter and timer on my wrist enabled me to make specific space-time readings during the descent, thus assuring this tape an invaluable and realistic continuity.

This, then, is what the long fall of Excelsior III was to me . . . .]

CHUTE OPENED

. . . Sixteen seconds after leaving the gondola. I feel the timer fire, then the jolt in my back as the timer yanks the cable to release the pack pins. I hear a muffled sound as it fires, and at this instant I suck in deeply, gratefully of air. It is my first breath since stepping away from the gondola.

STARTING TO PULL

As the timer fires, I grasp the ripcord to open the parachute manually if this proves necessary. This is my call that I have the ripcord in my left hand; it is impossible to use my right. But I never pull the ripcord; there is no need to do so.

THIRTY SECONDS

I read off the time from the stopwatch on my wrist. From here on I study the stopwatch and altimeter almost continuously . . . everything that happens to me must correlate to time and altitude. This is the key to gaining specific data, and lends full meaning to my spoken words. Thus, the stopwatch and the altimeter become a guide for my reports. But more important to me—for at this moment I am passing through 90,000 feet, and falling with the awesome speed of 614 miles per hour—this is my total world, my only link with reality.

MULTISTAGE IS WORKING PERFECTLY!

I feel the gentle tugging of Beaupre's stabilization parachute against the straps of my harness. It is the touch of an angel on my shoulder; a marvelous, exhilarating feeling . . . .

CAN'T GET MY BREATH . . .

Suddenly I feel as if I were being strangled by some invisible force! I knew this problem briefly during Excelsior II; we thought we had it whipped. But the strangling becomes worse . . . I fight desperately for air. Gray clouds swirl through my brain; I fear I will lose consciousness.

CAN'T GET MY . . . BREATH . . .

I am gasping. The choking sensation lasts for some 50 seconds total. Then the pressure vanishes. I breathe normally, am grateful.

STABILIZED PERFECT!

A ringing note of jubilation in my voice. I say to myself: *Thank you, Beau* . . . .

SEVENTY THOUSAND

One minute since leaving the gondola . . . with each sweep of the second hand an elation grows within me. It is not a conscious reaction, not a feeling of relief that I can define—or even try to. Just—something *wonderful*. Each second as I fall I race back into air closer to earth, air dense and rich and warm. It is a plunge back into the elixir of life . . . .

PERFECT STABILITY

As I fall, I make the most of the extraordinary stability of Beaupre's chute. I am able to start slowly to turn either to the right or to the left. These are the gentlest of motions. I use my feet as rudders . . . as I turn to the left, I lift my left foot slightly and roll (*not* a spin) stops. I start or stop motion any time I wish. The control I have is utterly fantastic! All this time the gentle tug on my shoulders continues. As I descend I begin to feel the effects of wind from the increasing density of air; the legs of my flying suit flutter in the wind like the rippling of a flag in a stiff breeze . . . . My earphones reduce the sound of the wind to the barest whisper (the tape recording, however, reveals the noise of the wind as a constant and very loud howl).

BEAUTIFUL!

How perfect a jump can be! Everything is going beautifully! I am almost wild with elation!

MINUTE AND THIRTY-FIVE SECONDS

Getting closer and closer to earth. No! More important, I am rapidly leaving the hostile environment. That matters more than being closer to earth . . . . The peak of danger is now ninety-five seconds *above* me.

MULTISTAGE . . . BEAUTIFUL STABILITY

Everything working flawlessly. I think of the horror I knew on the first Excelsior jump. How incredibly different, how perfect this is . . . .

MULTISTAGE PERFECT

It is simply incredible; what a magnificent experience!

SIXTY THOUSAND

Everything is going perfectly . . . .

(Two unintelligible statements)

FIFTY THOUSAND

My body has decelerated now from its peak speed of 614 miles per hour true airspeed at 90,000; my speed is now 250 miles per hour. I am back—with incredible ease—at that altitude I marked on my ascent as the beginning of the area of no return. Here is where I felt the failure of the glove, the onslaught of fear. Now I know only jubilation . . . even if the pressure suit fails, I am within a reasonably dense atmosphere. I continue to fall, so that within seconds I will no longer require body pressurization. I am back in the safer zone of flight where the flow of pure oxygen suffices to keep me alive and conscious during the continuing free-fall.

PERFECT STABILITY

It is a flawless descent . . . .

I'M GOING TO TURN TO THE RIGHT

I'm getting cocky now; I experiment again to see just what I can really do with this amazing parachute. I know I can stop any turning. Now I want to see just how much control I can get while making stronger, deliberate motions. I face toward the south, toward Texas. I start into a right turn; I want to look north toward Albuquerque.

BEAUTIFUL

I stop right on the button! I am exactly where I wish to be. What marvelous control!

PERFECT

It is simply fabulous . . . the control is almost impossible to believe . . . .

FACE PLATE GETTING FOGGED UP

I am passing through the coldest regions of the atmosphere; I fall through air that is 98 degrees below zero. Because of the rapid dissipation of the mask heat from windblast, thin edges of fog start to form on the sides and bottom of the faceplate.

FORTY THOUSAND

Coming down!

TWO MINUTES THIRTY SECONDS

It seems impossible that I have been falling this long. Everything is going so beautifully!

OUT OF POSITIVE PRESSURE

No more constriction.

THE FACEPLATE FOGGED UP A LITTLE BIT

THIRTY-FIVE THOUSAND

I check my altimeter more frequently . . . main canopy scheduled to go at 18,000.

(Unintelligible statement)

LITTLE COLD IN MY LEGS

THIRTY THOUSAND

NO . . . CORRECTION: THIRTY FOUR

COMING UP ON THREE MINUTES

PERFECT STABILITY!

FACEPLATE'S GETTING FOGGED UP . . . TAKING OFF MY SUN VISOR

CAN'T GET IT LOOSE

HERE WE GO–IT'S OFF

MAYBE THAT WILL HELP

AWFUL BRIGHT

THIRTY THOUSAND

THREE MINUTES THIRTY SECONDS

UNDERCAST BENEATH ME

Now the clouds—so remote a short time ago—rush rapidly toward me. I have never before dropped in a free-fall into clouds. I reassure myself that they are vapor and not the unyielding earth.

PERFECT STABILITY!

OVERRIDE IN MY HAND

FOR THE PACK OPENING

COMING UP ON TWENTY THOUSAND!

MULTISTAGE IS BEAUTIFUL . . . PERFECT STABILITY

FOUR MINUTES!

THE UNDERCAST BENEATH ME

THE MULTISTAGE IS GOING PERFECT . . . . BEAUTIFUL!

FOUR MINUTES TEN SECONDS

I CAN TURN AROUND PERFECT

CAN DO EVERYTHING

TWENTY THOUSAND

FOUR MINUTES TWENTY-FIVE SECONDS

FOUR MINUTES THIRTY SECONDS

WE'RE GOING INTO THE OVERCAST . . .

INTO THE OVERCAST!

THE MAIN CHUTE JUST OPENED ... RIGHT ON THE
BUTTON!

FOUR MINUTES AND THIRTY—SEVEN SECONDS
FREE-FALL

EIGHTEEN THOUSAND FEET

AHHH BOY!

THANK YOU, GOD, THANK YOU

THANK YOU FOR PROTECTING ME DURING THAT LONG
DESCENT

THANK YOU, GOD

THANK YOU ...

Kittinger's jump was to test gear only; setting any records was an incidental part of the project. Later, a sport jumper, Nick Piantanida attempted to surpass Kittinger's record. In fact, Kittinger and Piantanida set curious records of sorts, speaking strictly in numbers and physics; both men went over the sound barrier—without the comfortable surroundings of an airplane. Yet Piantanida's jumps were, in Kittinger's words, *a hostile arena*. Three times Piantanida attempted a record. On the third time, his equipment malfunctioned and he died in the attempt.

Kittinger's last duty station as an active Air Force officer was with the Twelfth Air Force, Bergstrom Air Force Base, Austin, Texas. Interviewed in his plush Austin suburban home in 1978, Kittinger, tranquilly recalling his jumps, is engaging, quick to smile, quick to give credit to his jump team. He has a shock of brown hair; if it were several shades lighter, Kittinger would be one of those men forever called "Red" by his colleagues. He spoke modestly of his achievements.

"Colonel Paul Stapp, the man who first made tests on a rocket sled to experiment with a pilot's physiological means to withstand shock, was the bravest man I have ever met. He showed me the knowledge, will and desire to succeed. He was a visionary. Progress is always measured in small increments. Itty-bitty steps. I was fortunate to advance our knowledge by making one of those small steps."

One could not help but recall Neil Armstrong's words, upon reaching the ageless dust of the moon, "That was one small step for man, one giant leap for mankind." Perhaps Col. Kittinger was thinking the same thoughts.

Curiously, Kittinger has few remnants of his jumping career. Asked to see his jump logbook, Kittinger took a long time to find it. It was an old 100-jump log, battered and bent beyond reason. It too, told a curious and fascinating story. Jumps were logged at infrequent intervals, in fits and starts, in strange locales: El Centro, California; Wright Patterson Air Force Base, Ohio; near Lake Erie; Elgin Air Force Base; Holloman Air Force Base; in Germany; in Norway; and at Lakeheath, England. Tucked into his jump log was a free balloonist's license; Kittinger had experience in hot air and gas balloons, as part of his training for the high altitude jumps.

Kittinger's jumps read like a log of military service craft. He has jumped from a UT Courier; an L20; a C 47 (DC-3); C 119; C 45 (D 18 Beech); C 123; a Beaver, and other aircraft with exotic and mysterious military designations.

One of his last jumps was the most poignant in his log. Kittinger listed a jump from an "F 4"; under "Type of Jump" he wrote "Eject"; and under "Comments," he wrote: *Unfriendly ground party.*

Col. Kittinger had been captured by the North Viet Namese and spent two and one-half years as a prisoner of war during the Viet Namese Conflict.

F 4. Eject. Unfriendly ground party.

For his work in the high altitude test, for his service career and for his bravery, Kittinger has a chest full of awards: he wears the Silver Star with one oak leaf cluster; the Legion of Merit; the Distinguished Flying Cross with five oak leaf clusters; the Purple Heart with one cluster; the Air Force Commendation Medal; the Viet Nam service medal with two service stars; and the Republic of Viet Nam Campaign Medal.

Among his awards, he won the Harmon International Trophy, presented to him by President Eisenhower in September, 1960; the Leo Stevens Parachute Medal; and the Wingfoot

Lighter-Than-Air Society Achievement Award (among others). He also holds over 7,000 hours of flight time, in 25 different kinds of Air Force aircraft.

One of his last jumps was a demo jump at Bergstrom Air Force Base, about 1977. A sport jump. A fun jump; 10,000 feet or so, with other Air Force sport jumpers. Kittinger jumped a rag chute. Others around him jumped squares. StratoStars, StratoClouds, ParaFoils. Kittinger was awed by them. He calls them *mattresses*.

"You know," he said, gazing toward the ceiling of his Austin home, "I'd have a lot of trouble with one of those mattresses." He paused a long time, perhaps thinking of blue skies and jumping, of perhaps what it was like from 76,000 feet, perhaps what the world looked like from 102,800 feet. What his own breathing sounded like in his helmet. Perhaps what he felt. What his own heartbeat felt like.

Col. Kittinger, the novice jumper, finally looked back. "I sure couldn't jump one of those mattresses without lots of help . . . ."

*From stunt jumping
in "The Gypsy Moths" to the
United States Parachute Association's
Board of Directors.
This is . . .*

Jerry Rouillard's Story

Like so many others in jumping, men and women, Jerry Rouillard's curiosity was piqued when he read about barnstorming jumpers. He remembers an article he read once in *Reader's Digest*. He was twelve at the time. "I was fascinated. The article had a tremendous impact on me. I knew when I was twelve that I wanted to have something to do with parachuting . . ."

He got his chance later, in the Army Airborne, in 1958, and completed 16 static line jumps. Later, at Arizona State University, he watched sport skydiving for the first time at the Deer Valley Airport, near Phoenix. "I wanted to make a sport jump then," Jerry says, "and the owner dug around in a closet until he found a packed rig. He put it on my back on the way to the plane . . .

"I learned about canopy control on my way down . . ."

His first sport jump, in 1963, led to twelve in the fall of 1964. He organized the Sun Devils Skydivers in the fall of 1964 and that club, which existed only one year, consisted of himself, Gary Lewis, who eventually worked for ParaGear Equipment Company in Chicago, John Lee who owned the Spring Creek, Texas parachute center before being killed in an aircraft accident in late 1978, and Sharon Clark, who eventually had over 700 jumps, also began her career with the Sun Devils Skydivers. Rouillard (pronounced *Rue*-lard) "supported my habit" by training students during the weekends.

By 1966, Jerry got his first film-making job involving an industrial company which involved a parachute jump. In 1967, he participated in a film which was used by dealers to introduce the 1967 line of Dodge cars. He earned enough to pay his way to California, where he bought a used PC and entered the next Conference meet. He won it and, with 220 jumps, entered the Nationals, held that year in Tahlequah, Oklahoma.

"I was lucky to be able to hit my ass with both hands," he said of that National competition. With 220 jumps, he was one of the least experienced competitors in the Nationals.

In the summer of 1966—and in the summer of 1967—he lucked into a job in the Wisconsin Dells Vacationland, making demonstration jumps into a sand beach "no larger than your front yard." It was the kind of jumping that quickly made a veteran out of a weekend jumper. "We jumped three times a day—if we didn't jump we didn't get paid. We—three of us—eventually got so good that we made 96 percent of our scheduled jumps. In Wisconsin weather—that's good. We learned how to do three-mans from 4,500 feet. We hit the beach most of the time too, but I've landed in back yards and made some accidental water jumps, during those demos."

Jerry went back to Arizona State for the fall of 1966, but the pull of skydiving was, by then, too strong. He left Arizona in the spring of 1967 because he knew the best jumping was California sunshine jumping. He moved to Oceanside, because that was closest to the best competition drop zone in California and got a job on the Oceanside police force. He graduated from the Police Academy in San Diego and was on the police force two weeks when Carl Boenish called. Boenish had known of Jerry's film work and demonstration jumping in an age when demos were rare—and Boenish called to say that a film "The Gypsy Moths" was beginning production.

"They needed someone with plenty of experience in demo jumping, whose record at jumping was good and they needed someone 'over six feet tall' to double for Burt Lancaster in the film. I quit the police force and headed for Kansas, where the film was beginning production. I was originally to have a two-week job with the film company. They needed good accuracy jumpers. The film stretched into two and one-half months and extra time after that in post-production work in the studios in California."

"The Gypsy Moths" employed six stunt jumpers: Jerry, Mike Milts, Garth Taggart, Russ Benefield, Dave Thompson, and Bill Ledbetter. Jerry Helms was their rigger and Carl Boenish and Jay Gifford were the aerial cameramen for the skydiving sequences.

"The only thing I ever regretted about making the film was the fact that it blew me out of the 1968 Nationals—I was working on the film all summer."

Produced by Robert Evans and directed by John Frankenheimer, "The Gypsy Moths" has served as introduction to skydiving for many modern sky divers since its release in 1969.

"I eventually did about 125 jumps for the film," Jerry says. "We did batwing jumps from 10,000 feet. The batwings were actually outlawed by then, but the U.S.P.A. and the F.A.A. were ready to give us a waiver of the rules for the jumps but Boenish forgot to ever apply for the waiver, so the batwing jumps were actually illegal. They weren't dangerous only awkward; they were uncomfortable jumps—we had a lot of gear on and two reserves—a piggyback reserve and a

Leaders in the Sport 169

Jerry Rouillard and his distinctive beard are well-known nationally. (photo courtesy of Jerry Rouillard)

front-mount reserve. In all, there were 1,200 jumps made for the film. During the film-making, on one occasion, I was doubling for Gene Hackman and I was supposed to 'fall' out of a plane, wearing a parachute concealed under a Brooks Brothers' suit. During the 'dummying' for the take, I was held in place on the edge of the door, with a static line, attached to the airframe with a quick-release snap. Two other stuntmen crawled over me and out the door. I was left hanging half in and half out because the plane was in a stall for exits. Afterward, the pilot said, 'if you had fallen out any farther, I'd have let you go by releasing the snap.' I told him, 'I'm glad you didn't, I wasn't wearing a chute.' He turned white."

"The Gypsy Moths" was a remarkable jump film, as much for what was never shown as for the skydiving sequences which were part of the finished film. "One of the officials, Robert Evans I think, had seen a sequence of Soviet jumpers pretending to play musical instruments in free-fall. One had a trombone, one a saxophone, and the other a snare drum. Frankenheimer said *that* kind of stunt jumping was impossible. So they had a private bet. Three of us went up to duplicate the stunt. Why, I don't know because it didn't have any relation at all to the rest of the film. The sax was okay and the trombone was okay, but the snare drum was impossible. It was like balancing on a bubble. Garth Taggart tried it and fell out of control for 45 seconds; he got scared of the jump and passed the drum on to Russ Benefield. He jumped with the drum attached to his front tie-downs, with a piggy-back reserve. The drum made him do unintentional backloops. He hurt his neck jumping with it and passed the stunt on to me. I put on heavy batwings and discovered that if the drum began to throw me to the left, I could correct to the right by extending the right bells and suit webbing. We finally got a 20-second shot, but I found that if the drum threw me unstable, the only way I could correct was by a head-down dive. The shot was never used."

Rouillard and the others also made a different shot which looked so patently false that it was never used.

"We tried a stunt that involved landing on a *moving* flatbed trailer, pulled along the airport runway. We did the shot twice—a third time one of the jumpers overshot and landed in a sandpit at the edge of the runway. Another jumper came in too low and hit the side of the truck. Even the best shot of that looked unbelievable, so that was never used."

Rouillard spent all summer in the midwest and then finished the filming in northern California. The trees in the midwest turned colors in the autumn and the film company had to find a location where the green matched the earlier footage of Kansas meadows.

"I have been asked since 'The Gypsy Moths' was released, why I wanted to be a part of that, since there was a skydiving suicide in the film and it didn't portray skydiving in such an appealing way. I was never too happy with that part of the theme either, but the film would have been made whether I was a part of it or not, and I was glad to be a part of the skydiving sequences to make them as accurate as possible."

He made enough from the film-making to take "the rest of the year off. I bought a new ParaCommander, a motorcycle and a van—I put my dog in the van and jumped all over."

By the end of August 1969, his film money gone, Rouillard moved to Monterey, California, to become Assistant Director of the United States Parachute Association, under Norman Heaton. For two and one-half years, Rouillard coordinated the National Collegiate Parachuting League, helped run *Parachutist* magazine and eventually worked on all phases of the U.S.P.A.

After working on three national collegiate meets, one involving over 200 college sky divers, meeting a cross-section of U.S.P.A. members, Rouillard returned to San Diego, to join the staff of the Federal Defender and begin law school at night. That career lasted from the middle of 1971 to May 1973.

"I really didn't mind the job of investigator, but I had seen enough of the law to know that I didn't want to spend the rest of my life in the middle of lawyers," he now says.

After attending the 1973 Nationals, he got a call. Would he become team leader for the U. S. team, going to the Adriatic Cup in Europe?

"I was easy to convince; everyone knew I was 'at liberty' —jobless—so from July to September of 1973, we helped train the team. We took it to Europe and entered the Adriatic Cup and brought it back on $6,000. It was the first and only chance Betsy Robson and some others had to enter international competition so I was happy to go to help some of the nationally-known jumpers have a shot at international competition . . ."

The Adriatic Cup is something of an odd international event. In addition to style and accuracy, it also involved a water jump—sky divers must land as close as possible to a buoy, ditch their gear and swim to another buoy, an odd and nearly useless event.

"Gary Lewis was the team coach and he read all the results and knew from previous years that we couldn't improve our chance much in the training period we had, in the style and accuracy. He and I knew that if our people didn't have enough talent in style and accuracy, we couldn't teach them well in a few weeks. So we concentrated on the water jump. We trained every day—they—the team members swam like fish every day, in the morning and the evening. They swam out of parachute gear, they swam through canopies in a pool, they swam for speed and distance.

"When we got to the competition, the Russians had a coach who was a full-time skydiving coach. They were ahead in the style and accuracy competitions. But not by much. Their coach was smiling—he thought he had the whole program wrapped up. We blew everyone away in the water jump. Simply blew everyone away. Our people won it all. The poor Russian coach looked like he'd been pole-axed. We had won a minor meet and a huge moral victory . . ."

After bringing home the U. S. team, Jerry looked around, did some jumping here and there and was enchanted with a small DZ in Roanoke Rapids, North Carolina. He borrowed all he could and bought it and ran it for a year and a half, from late 1973 to early 1975. He also began working for The Chute Shop in New Jersey, selling gear and, more importantly, developing the reefing system for the ParaFoil, one of the first exceptional ram-air or square parachutes. (Prior to the development of the ParaFoil and StratoStar, the earlier ram-airs such as the VolPlane and the ParaSled had enormous opening shocks. The ParaFoil was one of the first to use a delayed system which helped control opening shock to make the parachute appealing to sport jumpers.)

He moved his Roanoke Rapids DZ to Suffolk, Virginia

Without his beard, Jerry is fitted for a stunt jump with a break-away Brooks Brothers suit, during the filming of "The Gypsy Moths." (photo courtesy of Jerry Rouillard)

in 1975, to be closer to The Chute Shop, only to return to Virginia in 1976 when profits of the Suffolk operation were declining. He sold out from under a still-declining operation and surveyed how and where to begin again. He chose the Sunbelt and believed his best chances were in a place where economics and weather made jumping congenial. He finally narrowed his choices to Dallas, Houston, or San Antonio, and moved to Dallas, where he began working for McElfish and gauging the Texas climate and heritage and jumping systems.

He finally began his Lake Lavon Parachute Center, now called Skydivers of Texas, Inc., outside Dallas, in 1977, with a Cessna 182 and a complete new generation of interested Texas sky divers.

By 1979, Jerry Rouillard has had 22 years in sport parachuting (he was 38 as this book went to press). With his Texas DZ, he began new techniques, new ideas, and new styles of operation.

"We wanted to get away from the old 'eat, sky dive and screw' type of jumper. We have a new crew of affluent weekend jumpers without fixed ideas and interested in learning. We now charge for what other DZ's give away—we offer a complete schedule of earned achievements to keep new jumpers interested in their own progress; we charge $6 for a packing class so they don't pick up packing techniques the wrong way; we offer a spotting class after their first free-fall but before their 30-second delays. I was reluctant at first to charge for that, but I discovered that when we began the class, a lot of our older jumpers hung around the edge of the class, so now we offer it on a regular basis. We offer a Free-fall Techniques class for $10 and a one-on-one Relative Work class. We don't want the type of operation that lets a free-fall jumper with 15 jumps go base for a four-man attempt. What happens if these novice people can't hold a heading? What happens if they panic? We don't want that type of situation. So we program all our new people and don't get them into that too-soon-too-fast situation . . ."

Jerry Rouillard now has his Senior Rigger's license, Instrument and Commercial Pilot's licenses, SCR No. 139, 'D' license No. 2500 and "quit logging jumps five years ago at 2,900." He now believes that he has about 4,000 jumps. He has never applied for his SCS because he believes "that award encourages sloppy jumping. Someone exits third and comes in (into a star) eighth and gets his SCS. I don't believe in that . . ."

He served on the United States Parachute Association

nationally-elected Board of Directors for five years, declining to run for re-election at the end of his term in late 1978.

The innovations he has established at his DZ, innovations which make new novice jumpers "involved in their own fate" and "informed in techniques and gear" mark him many steps higher psychologically than the average DZ operator, who is interested in keeping his planes in the air, keeping the F.A.A. off his neck and stopping the bitching from the skygods in residence. Jerry Rouillard frankly and unabashedly caters to his novice jumpers and, as a logical result, has a crew of enthusiastic jumpers, all progressing safely and congenially toward being skygods. There is surprisingly little bitching at his DZ, much encouragement of positive work. "We have had to tell some people that they would be happier jumping elsewhere," he says, "but we haven't had to say that very often. The dirty-T-shirt crowd soon gets the message . . ."

In national skydiving circles, Jerry Rouillard is, with his full red-brown beard, certainly one of the most recognizable jumpers in the country. Only Al "Captain Hook" Krueger is as recognizable.

She has organized the most famous women's skydiving team in sport parachuting. This is the story of . . .

jeanni McCombs and the Star Dusters

She has been a parachute test jumper, the first woman to reach 24 hours of total free-fall time and one of the few women in sport parachuting to own her own parachute supply company. But jeanni McCombs is perhaps best known for the leadership she has exerted in women's parachuting and, since 1970, her team, the Star Dusters, has been one of the premier demonstration teams in the country.

Like Jerry Rouillard and Al Krueger, jeanni began her own

career in sport parachuting out of idle curiosity, watching a friend make a few jumps. It was in 1960 in El Paso; the friend, making the jumps, was having a good time. jeanni, watching from the ground, was not having a good time. A Jumpmaster finally asked her if she'd like to make a jump. She did and made five static line jumps. She then broke her neck in an automobile accident and not until 1961 did she begin again in sport parachuting.

By 1962, jeanni was good enough to attend the Nationals, held that year at Olathe, Kansas. She won the women's accuracy championships that year too; she learned how by jumping with men. "I had never jumped with women," she now says, "I think that makes you naturally better. The men knew everything about jumping and winds. I learned about winds by flying kites. I think that competing with men makes you better in any sport."

She was part of the ten-woman delegation for the 1962 U. S. Team which was the host team for the 1962 World Meet, held at Orange, Massachusetts.

In 1964, she was part of the three-woman delegation from the U. S. which flew to Yugoslavia for the World Meet. Annie Batterson and Carolyn Olson were other women's team members.

In 1964, she was also part of the U. S. delegation to the World Meet, held that year in West Germany. "The U. S. took second place that year—1964 was the year that the East Germans began coming out of the woodwork," she says.

She had moved from Texas to California in 1963, and by 1964, jeanni was traveling throughout the state selling advertising for various Chambers of Commerce. She also got a chance to jump at all of the DZs in California. In 1964, she began test jumping, as the only woman testing the Rogallo-shaped Delta II parachute for the Irving Parachute Company.

"You had to wear a mouthguard for the Delta II," she now says, "the opening shock was terrific. It was almost impossible to stabilize the Delta II; after opening, it surged forward, then the jumper swung forward under the canopy, then the Delta surged forward again. Once it began this, there was no way to stop it. I hand-deployed a reserve six times trying to stop the Delta II." After that test series, jeanni

jeanni McCombs and Becky Livingston at the Reno Air Races. (Kathy Ryan photo)

appeared on "To Tell the Truth." Artistically, the show was a disaster. "I coached two housewives in parachute language and techniques before the show, but both of them were shorter than I was. The producers dressed them in painter's coveralls. I was the only one on the show who looked healthy and athletic—the panelists guessed me immediately."

"To Tell the Truth" not withstanding, jeanni has been part of the United States Nationals every year since 1962 (except for two years) and has always placed in the top five or ten in women's competition.

"I never really competed to win. I like RW. For two weeks prior to each Nationals, I practice style and accuracy so I wouldn't make a fool of myself . . .

"The Nationals are a homecoming to me . . . I love them all . . ."

In 1965, jeanni organized her first women's team, The Lady Bugs. "We did commercials for exterminators—we killed the bad guys . . ." With help from Bob Sinclair, one of the premier California parachute officials in those days (he helped Johnny Carson make Carson's celebrated 12,500 foot first jump free-fall), jeanni and the Lady Bugs began making exhibition jumps for charity. The J. Walter Thompson advertising agency also helped with advertising and promotion.

By 1964, she took her first women's team to the Reno Air Races, now the only air races in the United States. jeanni McCombs has had the only non-airplane part of the air races and the only all women's exhibition.

After her first year, her schedule of exhibitions is most impressive: she has jumped into the Los Angeles Coliseum (1964) with an Olympic flag to celebrate the beginning of the 1964 Mexico City Olympics; she opened the Anaheim Convention Center in 1965 with an exhibition jump carrying a 9 by 12 foot flag. ("That flag was so heavy—it was made of four thicknesses of cloth—that every time I dropped it and let it unfurl, it began to collapse my chute. I had to pull it up to let the chute deploy—if I dropped it the chute would collapse again . . . But I made the jump . . .") She opened the Berkeley Marina in 1967 with a water jump into the Marina and, in 1970, organized The Star Dusters, since that time the best-known women's exhibition team in the country.

"We have continued to do the air shows," she says, "we have traditionally opened the Reno Air Races. We have been sponsored recently by Levis and Puma racing shoes. I pick girls who not only can jump, but who are attractive and who can wear clothes well and smile all day. We generally jump three to five girls or more for exhibition, but have jumped as many as 11 during one show."

Betsy Robson, one of the Star Dusters, continued with the team until her work took her to Washington, D.C. She later became one of the U.S.P.A. Board of Directors.

jeanni's pilot has been Tim Saltenstall, once owner of the

Leaders in the Sport 179

jeanni and The Star Dusters. Left to right, Betsy Robson, Virginia Romaine, jeanni, Lisa McCombs Gardner, Kathy Drag, and Cynthia Fruch. (Kathy Ryan photo)

Pope Valley Parachute Ranch, in California. With 3,000 jumps of his own, Saltenstall is a most trusted jump pilot and now owns the DC-3 which flies at Pope Valley.

"We don't use women who are competitive jumpers," she says, "we want girls who are outdoor entertainers, who get along, who jump well." During the three-day Reno Air shows, jeanni and the Star Dusters will compete three different routines and wear three different outfits. One day's program might be two girls doing a two-person star, jeanni flying a square with a U. S. flag and two more girls jumping with smoke on their boots. The Star Dusters are an accomplished and professional exhibition team.

Personally, jeanni has accomplished almost as much as anyone can accomplish in American sport parachuting. She received her U.S.P.A. 'B' (No. 987) and 'C' (No. 709) in 1961; her 'D' (No. 251) in 1962. She received SCR No. 77 although she did participate in the first SCR attempt ever made. With 2,700 jumps as this book goes to press, she holds her 24-hour free-fall badge (No. 35—the first woman to achieve that award) and is working on her Double Diamond Wings (3,000 jumps) award.

"I've never really tried to be first in anything, but I have been in the sport for 18 years now (in 1979) and have logged all my jumps. I have my logbooks in a safety deposit box because they are such a crucial part of my life . . ."

All the members of The Star Dusters jump parachutes of their own choosing. Some jump StratoClouds and some jump StratoStars. jeanni jumps the Unit parachute system.

"The Star Dusters will remain an exhibition team—we actively seek sponsorship and exhibition dates, but we are not a competitive team. We are all strictly fun jumpers who are into RW jumping."

She has been in a 36-person star and has made all the loads leading toward women's world record attempts. "In 1976, I once made five jumps with a cast on my leg—it was important to me to make those jumps. I once sprained an ankle and *stopped jumping one whole day.* I finally said the heck with it and got back into it the next day."

In April of 1978, jeanni was invited by California Governor Jerry Brown to represent the parachuting community at the first official launching of the space shuttle Enterprise. jeanni was invited to all the governmental luncheons and celebrations. "It was fun talking with all those astronauts and people," she says. "We planned originally to jump into the opening ceremonies but that was well, abandoned eventually."

Now 48, jeanni has been jumping since she was 29. She has devoted a larger part of her life to sport parachuting than many of her contemporaries; many of her early jump partners have long since left the sport. She continues, not only as well, but better than she did in the early days. She now sells the G. Q. Security parachute line although she doesn't have a rigging license. "I hand all that (rigging) to other people," and her advertisements can be seen in major parachuting magazines, such as *Spotter* and *Parachutist.* Just like Jerry Rouillard, whom she has known for years, she has begun to sell gear to help support her skydiving habit.

She now owns her own Victorian brownstone near the California coast and jumps at Pope Valley. She foresees no end to The Star Dusters. She has not lost touch with the times. Her Security dealership helps her stay current with

jeanni McCombs, with a square parachute and a smoke bomb, at the Reno Air Races. (Kathy Ryan photo)

trends in skydiving. She has now begun to compete in the ParaSki accuracy and skiing competitions held annually during the winter. "I'm really not good yet at skiing, I get afraid going that fast so close to the ground, but I'm an ace with accuracy, jumping my square . . ."

jeanni has naturally curly ringlets of brown hair surrounding sparkling eyes. When she looks at you, she means what she says, as many male jumpers have learned . . . "I'll never give up jumping . . . it's been the balance point in my life."

*At 57, George McCulloch was called
a 'Bold American.'
Now, well past 70, he is even bolder.
For George, his wife Harriet and others their age,
parachuting is not just for the young . . .*

George and Harriet McCulloch's Story

You could look it up.

There on the cover of the December 24, 1962 issue of *Sports Illustrated* was George McCulloch skydiving. The cover story, "The Bold American," profiled young athletes involved with unusual or exceptional sports. There were features on white-water canoeing, cave exploring, glider pilots, mountain climbing, and ballooning. On a two-page spread was a photograph of George, exiting a jump plane, over Orange, Massachusetts. The caption read, "George McCulloch, 57, Commissioner of Urban Improvement for Syracuse, improves his morale by skydiving. 'A great relief from the pressures of my job,' he said happily, before plummeting out the door."

Now, well over 70, George is still happily "plummeting" out of the doors of jump planes, only now it's no longer a relief from his job. George is retired, but he acts like no senior citizen you've ever seen.

Since his 60th birthday (July 4, 1965), he has celebrated by making a birthday skydive and falling in free-fall one second for each year he is old. At the end of the count, he opens his parachute. Since his 60th birthday, he has added a second for each additional year, although normally a 60-second delayed-opening free-fall jump is the highest sport jumpers usually go.

"As an old newsman, I thought the idea of 60 (seconds) at 60 (years) was a good idea. Each year since, we've added the extra second. It was always fun and some years we've added something else too."

His logbooks show great dedication in pursuit of his sport; George has consistently (although sometimes doggedly), year after year, averaged 50 jumps per year. As you read this,

Leaders in the Sport 183

George will probably have made his 1,000th jump to receive the coveted "Gold Wings" from the U.S.P.A.

The following summaries of his "birthday jumps" are excerpted from his logbooks.

Year	Birthday	Place	Altitude	Aircraft	Jump No.	Comments
1965	60th	Orange, Mass.	12,500	Norseman	148	25 yds. out
1966	61st	Turners Falls, Mass.	12,800	Howard	205	Tree landing
1967	62nd	Turners Falls, Mass.	13,000	Howard	262	Out (100 yds.) 2-man hookup
1968	63rd	Turners Falls, Mass.	13,500	Cessna 182	308	12 yds. Missed 2-man
1969	64th	Turners Falls, Mass.	13,500	Cessna 182	340	Missed 2-man
1970	65th	Turners Falls, Mass.	13,500	Cessna 182	434	15 yds. 2-man
1971	66th	Fulton, NY	13,700	C 170	512	2-man hookup
1972	67th	Seneca Falls, NY	14,000	C 182	568	Out 2-man hookup
1973	68th	Seneca Falls, NY	14,000	C 182	627	Out 2 2-man hookups
1974	69th	Seneca Falls, NY	14,000	C 182	671	4 meters missed 2-man
1975	70th	Seneca Falls, NY	11,500	C 182	722	Failed to get altitude; jumped lower than desired
1976	71st	Fulton, NY	17,760 (This is approx. 90 second delay)	Cessna 206	759	Bicentennial jump. Higher altitude than needed to reach 1776(0) Chuck Schmutz made jump No. 1,776 on load
1977	72nd	Durhamville, NY	15,000	C-180	786	Two man. Third jumper missed. Wore smoke.

1978 (July 1)	73rd	Durhamville, NY	15,700	Beaver	847	Double Birthday jump. Got 3-man.
(July 4)		Willow Grove Naval Air Station, Pa.			(Attended 2nd birthday jump in a Sky Van with United Parachute Club, of New Hanover, Pa., but grounded by rain.)

The "something else" at his 69th birthday was a planned 69-mile bicycle ride, followed by the 69-second delayed opening free-fall jump.

George and a friend, Hubert (Huey) Parrow, began the 47-mile bicycle ride from Syracuse, New York, through Auburn, New York, to their DZ at Seneca Falls, New York, early on the morning of July 3. To make the full 69 miles, George planned to ride *through* Seneca Falls, pedal an additional 11 miles and return to the Seneca Falls airport, where the Seneca Falls Sport Parachute Club drop zone is located. George had a flat tire past Auburn while spelling Huey on Parrow's bicycle. Parrow stayed on the road while George pedaled on to Seneca Falls. George and his wife Harriet returned to Parrow, who had fixed the tire himself and insisted on completing the ride to Seneca Falls. But with darkness approaching, the rest of the planned 69-mile trip was scratched.

When George and Huey returned to the DZ, Harriet had dinner ready on a Coleman stove beside their campus. "Just 22 more miles dear," George said.

"No, George, eat your dinner," Harriet told him, petulantly.

He did, reluctantly. "That George," Harriet later told friends, "when he gets an idea in his head, he's like a bulldog with a bone. He just won't let go of it."

To compensate for the lost 22 miles of the bicycle ride, George added a night jump to his program. In a full moon, he strapped a flashlight to his arm, added a flashing strobelight to his helmet and, at midnight, jumped from 8,000 feet with two parachutists barely a third his age, Paul Campbell, of Ithaca and Kim Allen, of Ovid, New York. George's jump was nearly perfect. He landed in a wheat field adjacent to the DZ.

Early on the morning of July 4, George, Pat Stone, of

Marion, New York, and Harriet along as a spectator, climbed into a Cessna 182, for the long climb to 14,200 feet—the calculated height needed for the 69-second delayed fall.

"The waiting in the airplane is the hardest part," George says. "It takes 45 minutes to one hour to get up to a jump height like 14,2; the Cessnas aren't supercharged and that engine grinds a long time to get there. I am a timid jumper and I always have been. I have to psych myself up for that long jump. The plane is cramped and I have a long time to think things over . . ."

George *has* had a long time to think things over and, like the bulldog Harriet mentioned, George seldom lets go of anything once he makes up his mind to do something.

Born in South Dakota, George grew up in Oswego, New York. He graduated in the Syracuse University class of '28 and, until World War Two (which George always refers to as "War Two") he was a city desk reporter for the Syracuse *Post-Standard*. He and Harriet were a Depression marriage and have no children. When "War Two" came, George was too old for the service but, in the line of duty, spent a year in the North Atlantic in the Merchant Marines. After that year, he was then able to talk his way into the service and joined the Air Force. He was sent into the intelligence service in the Pacific. Not willing to be left home alone, Harriet joined the WAVES and was a Link Trainer operator in Philadelphia. "For a while she outranked me," George laughs.

During his stay in the Pacific, George researched early activities in the war in the Pacific.

After the war, George saw how society was changing. He quit *The Post-Standard*, changed his life and began graduate school at the University of Wisconsin.

"My eyes were bad and Harriet had to do all my reading for me," he says. He received his Master's degree in regional planning (one of the first such degrees awarded) from Wisconsin in 1947.

He returned to New York and became the first Commissioner for Urban Development in Syracuse. In 1964, he became the Stamford, Connecticut, redevelopment coordinator and director of urban development. Three years later, working out of Hartford, Connecticut, he was appointed director in charge of the New Haven district for the Connecticut State Department of Community Affairs. He retired eventually and returned to Syracuse; his retirement, such as it is, is as active as his career was. He became a charter member of the Oswego County Pioneer Search and Rescue Team, a volunteer search unit and he was also Secretary of the New York State Federation of Search and Rescue Teams. For three years, he was the housing expert for ACCORD, a Syracuse-area senior citizens action group.

But in the Syracuse and central New York area—indeed throughout most of the United States—George and Harriet are known as the Grand Old Couple of Parachuting, senior citizens in a sport populated with athletes far, far younger then they.

As George says, "I got started in 1959. The parachuting center in Orange, Massachusetts, now one of the biggest and oldest in the country, began operations in April or May of 1959. I saw several magazine articles about it, including a major article in *Life* and got curious about it. It was a six- or seven-hour drive from Syracuse and there just weren't any jump zones closer. Or any superhighways, either, for that matter. Jacques Istel was running the Orange center then. He got me started in parachuting. I was scared as hell . . .

"I kept hoping a doctor would ground me. One did look at me. 'Your heart is pumping like mad and your blood pressure is up slightly, but you're okay to jump,' he said.

"Like the bumblebee the engineers say can't fly, but flies anyway, I was pretty clumsy. No one, including me, thought I could ever get the hang of it. Lew Sanborn, who holds a D No. 1 license (the first expert rating), advised Harriet I should try some other sport. I would have welcomed anything that would have taken me out of the sport . . . I'm not too courageous a guy . . ."

He was courageous enough to keep on jumping. When *Sports Illustrated* came to Orange for the 1962 feature "The Bold American," Jacques Istel pointed to his most tenacious pupil. It was a high compliment. Istel was held in such high esteem as a pioneer in sport parachuting that being a protege of his is comparable to learning baseball from Babe Ruth, or boxing from Joe Louis. Name your sport, the distinction's the same.

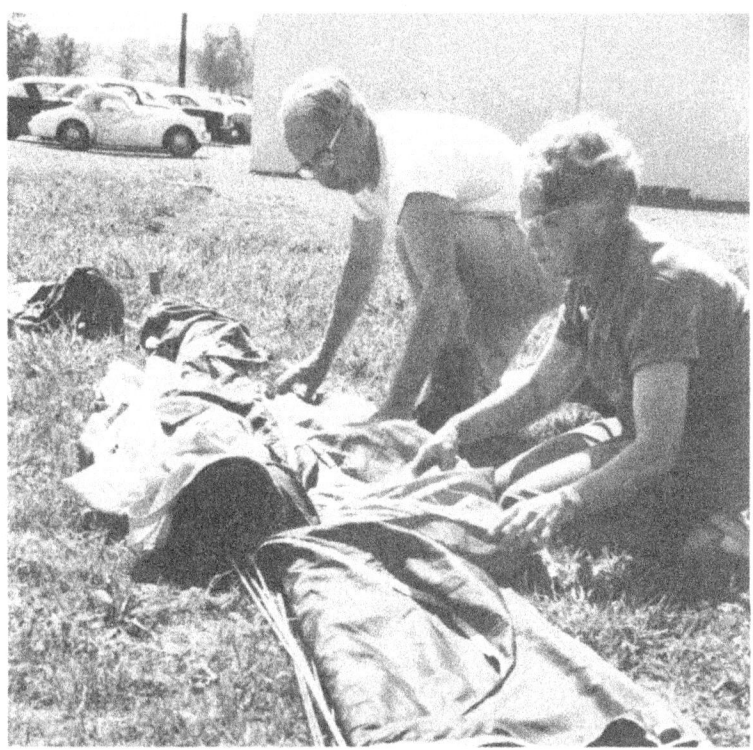

George and Harriet McCulloch, packing George's ParaCommander. No one packs more carefully than Harriet. (Thomas Fensch photo)

George and Harriet kept driving back and forth to Orange, sometimes making the long trip for the sake of one jump during a marginal jump weekend. When parachute centers began to spring up legally in New York state, they no longer had to make the long drive. But in 1969, before he retired and moved back to Syracuse, George had one of the most infamous jump experiences in U. S. sport parachute history — a jump which has to be the "ultimate jump story."

On October 25, 1969, he was jumping at the Turner's Falls, Massachusetts airport. An acquaintance, Marc James, was putting out a static line student at 5,200 feet, then he and George would make a two-man jump at 5,200 feet. The student exited on the static line, often called the "dope rope" by Jumpmasters and experienced jumpers. James exited and George quickly crawled through the plane for his jump. Usually the static lines are anchored to the airframe of the plane. On this flight, the Jumpmaster—James—had inadvertently hooked the static line to the coil spring of the pilot's seat.

As George hastily crawled through the 182, following James, the static line wrapped around George's leg. It knotted without his knowledge.

When he dove out the door, the static line tightened. He fell about eight feet and hung upside down under the door of the plane. He couldn't have reached the knot in the line and couldn't have untied it if he could have reached it. The pilot really didn't realize anything was wrong. George did the one thing possible: he pulled his main ripcord, hoping the opening shock of the parachute would snap the ring in the floor of the plane. It didn't but two other things happened instantaneously: he got a badly sprained ankle and the chute opening pulled the pilot's seat out the door of the plane!

George had always called the jump his "5,200-Foot Static Line Jump." He landed safely with his sprained ankle and with the pilot's seat dangling under it. The pilot, Fred Pease, landed the aircraft successfully by flying it from the floor, watching out the open jumpdoor, instead of through the windshield. From the ground, it appeared that the aircraft was landing itself, Pease was so invisible in the bowels of the 182.

George later signed an affidavit attesting to the truth of the incident. His affidavit was witnessed by the pilot and others at the dropzone at the time.

As the "ultimate jump accident," George's jump has been told and re-told, with varying degrees of accuracy, since. Without citing names, George's jump story appears in *The Jumpmaster's Handbook*, the officially-authorized guide to Jumpmaster training, distributed by the U.S.P.A.

J. Scott Hamilton, author of *The Jumpmaster's Guide*, retold George's story this way:

> Just recently, an experienced jumper up in New England encountered a similar horror show, except that he was jumping a fixed-wing aircraft and the pilot, not even noticing that he had a jumper in tow, did his customary wing-over into a steep spiral descent . . . heading for the ground. The hapless jumper, not having a knife, and unable to pull himself up the static line or

untie it, weighed his prospects of surviving a landing drag against the alternative of losing his foot, then reached in, gritted his teeth, and dumped his P.C.

He, too, received a larger share of luck than any mortal is authorized, for he was, in less than an instant, hanging under a properly inflated P.C., with a sprained ankle and the pilot's seat dangling eight feet below from the static line . . .

Harriet has jumped too, and has received her share of headlines. In the November 1966 issue of *Glamour* magazine, an article, "Swinging Sports," said:

> Part of the thrill of parachuting at first, is the challenge of one's own terror. Man or woman, you have to face yourself as you stand in front of the open door of the airplane. It's not that the sport is just for kicks, but a large part of the excitement is in proving that you too, can operate under stress.
>
> "Age and sex do not disqualify you from jumping. George McCulloch, a pupil of Istel's had made 200 jumps by his sixtieth birthday and still jumps regularly. For that matter, his wife took up parachuting at the age of 55, though she has since been grounded by her husband. "We've shared an awful lot of experiences together and she thought she'd see what it was like," Mr. McCulloch explained.

"She was a lot better at it than I was, at first," George now says. "She took to it right away. But it made me a nervous wreck. She made her first jump when I had hurt a foot in a landing accident. I was on crutches when she went up and I thought that would surely make her lose her nerve. It didn't faze her. It petrified me to watch her come down."

George was a bit of a male chauvinist before that term was known.

"Wives are not expendable. I asked her to stop. Now she helps me pack my parachute."

Usually Harriet does *most* of the packing, fretting and complaining when George seems more than a touch inept at it. Her example is usually not enough for younger women to emulate; younger men usually can't persuade their girlfriends or wives to pack as carefully as Harriet McCulloch.

Parachuting is a sport that demands much of the 'chutist. George has had his share of minor accidents. The sprained ankle at the Turners Falls incident, another broken foot during a landing accident and a cracked vertebra caused when he opened his reserve parachute while falling upside down; the opening shock whipped him right-side-up and cracked the vertebra. He also crushed two vertebrae several years ago in a POPS competition landing.

"Parachuting isn't something you get for free—if you want to do something bad enough, you eventually pay for it with an occasional small injury. Strictly speaking, parachuting isn't as dangerous as skiing," he says. (George is exactly right. His home dropzone of Orange, Mass., has posted a 2/10ths of one percent student injury rate since it opened; three fatalities since the late 1950s.)

Also George demurs about relative work—he does do RW frequently. He won his SCR award (March 5, 1978) jumping in Florida with members of POPS. Several articles were published after George's jump. It was unusual because of the ages and experience of all the jumpers in the star. One article, in *Spotter* magazine (May-June, 1978 issue), was typical of how George and his friends were treated:

> Eight-mans are a dime a dozen these days, as the stars get bigger and bigger. However, one was recently put together down in Eustis, Florida, which *might* be one for Guinness.
>
> The one was an eight-man POPSTAR. The Parachutists Over Phorty, that unique non-organization of "older" jumpers, had already made ten (8-or-more-men) POPSTARS, including one 11-man last year. But this one was a still a bit special. *Average age was 50-plus, and the ages ranged all the way from 41 to 72.*
>
> The 72-year-old (73 as of July 4th) thereby won his POPSTAR patch and his SCR.
>
> The "Old Timer" was George McCulloch of Syracuse (POPS No. 102), who flew base. Eleven POPS bombed out of a Twin Beech over Jimmy Godwin's Paragators DZ at 12,500 feet during the POPS' traditional "winter" meet in March. Tom Morrison, POPS 96, head man of United Parachutists at New Hanover, PA, pinned George in about five seconds; the star built to eight with about eight seconds to spare.
>
> In the star were: McCulloch, 72 (826 jumps); Morrison, 54 (2,868); Ex-TOPPOP Mike Efstration, 52 POPS No. 37 (1,340); Maximilian Miensopust, 47, No. 541 (2,090); Lew Sanborn, 47, No. 548 (1,926); Harry Ervin, 45, No. 661 (690); Jerry Thompson, 44, No. 692 (700); and Larry Cordeiro—a youngster of 41, No. 919 (1,367).

Four of the eight—Thompson, Morrison, Efstration, and Miensopust—were in the first POPSTAR four years ago.

Three guys went below: TOPPOP Bob Rhyne of Flint, Michigan, who was on the load despite a recent hernia operation, reputedly acquired from carrying the heavy TOPPOPS load (Bob reported he "just hung out there" as "Official Observer"); Dick Emerson (No. 1100) and Frank Gabriel (No. 831).

The ages of the eight men in the star totaled 402; total jumps—11,807 . . .

It was the Old Timer's (McCulloch's) 826th jump since he read about the opening of Orange, Mass., by P.I., 19 years ago. In the star was Lew Sanborn . . . Jacques Istel's partner when Orange opened, who signed off George's sixth jump back in 1959.

George was carried off the dropzone on the shoulders of all his friends and jumping buddies . . . holding George on his shoulders was Lew Sanborn, who told George to give up jumping, all those years ago, in Orange, so many jumps ago, when George plainly couldn't learn how to jump.

That "Old Timer," getting his SCR and his POPSTAR in his 70's . . . carried off the field in triumph, while Harriet had tears in her eyes . . . was given a black-and-gold jumpsuit with the SCR patch on one sleeve and POPS insignia—Father Time jumping in a rocking chair, white beard flowing in the wind, jumping hell-bent-for leather, pulling his ripcord with the handle of his walking cane . . . fingers crossed for good luck.

George is as proud as one patch as the other.

Friends later gave him framed photographs of the eight-man star, taken by free-fall photographer George Frey.

George and Harriet McCulloch, who have seen the beginning of sport parachuting in this country, when there was only one commercial dropzone . . . have seen their sport grow to 50-man stars out of SkyVans . . . have seen national conventions and gear generations and designs away from the "cheapos" he used to use in Orange . . . .

George, the old newspaperman, who has written a most evocative poem about jumping, unabashedly in rhyme:

> *He who climbs into a plane,*
> *And mounts into the blue,*
> *Then dives to dare the Sea of Air,*
> *Has joined the favored Few.*

> *Though his landing be with laughter—*
> *Though he seem like other men—*
> *He will never—ever after—*
> *Be the same again.*
>
> *He has climbed the cloudy Mountain—*
> *He has tasted of the fountain—*
> *He will never—ever after—*
> *Be the same again.*

(Complete poem in the Poetry section of this work.)

George and Harriet McCulloch . . . years older than the youngsters who are sky divers . . . and respected nationally in the sport. They have friends everywhere in U. S. parachuting.

When his friend and former mentor Jacques Istel learned of his birthday jumping, he wrote George a note: "All best wishes for your 90-second delay in a few years . . ."

When you're tired of all the hassles and the skygods, just . . .

Epilogue: Make a Skydive!

by Dean Frazier

When you find yourself dissatisfied with your jumping; when you make what technically could be called a good dive, but you feel not completely fulfilled; when you find yourself tiring of preoccupation with RW, the disc, CRW, style, students, your jump friends, the whole lot—take a minute to recall where you have come from, and what you do each time you go up and come down on "Wings of Flight." You may have fallen into the habit of fixed-action patterns in your pursuit of your sport. You may have lost some or all of the joy and thrill of those days when your spirit soared to undreamed-of heights, by the 'mere' act of making a skydive.

When your jumping sours, try this. Go back to basics. Go up, jump alone, take your time, and really sense your skydive. Enjoy the sky and earth while in the plane, unpreoccupied with what slot (when and where) you "have to be." Unbothered with overshooting the disc, not thinking of collapsing endcells, or if the student will tumble, or about anyone or anything but you and the sky and the earth and sea below. And when it's time to bail out (a rarely used phrase nowadays), have the pilot chop power if you're jumping a light plane, and make a poised exit. That's right, stand out on the step bracing against the strut just as you did a million years ago. And look around you. Look at the pilot, the sky and the land in front, the target area below, and out and away to the far horizons. Look at the region of time and space in which you play. Then cast off, and feel, drink in through all your named and unnamed senses, that time, that space.

Look around! Watch the changing panorama of sky and earth as you change your vantage point. How the size of distant objects changes, how the quality of their light-reflecting characteristic changes with altitude. Look at you! Look at your feet, your hands, your equipment, your clothing. See again the fury of rushing air unleashed by your penetration of the fluid medium. And when it's time (it may never be) to halt the downward plunge, take your time with throw-out or ripcord, feel what you are doing, grasp it, but hold it while you stabilize on one hand only. Had you forgotten how? Had you forgotten that you need to, lest you spin? Then, pull your legs together, bring your knees up, throw your head back, and finally release it, and watch, and listen, and see your parachute deploy! Forgotten how thrilling a sight it is up close? It says YES! It says NOW!

On canopy descent, forget for a moment about the target area, the disc (if safety allows the former), and let yourself drift. No fair playing with the control lines. Look around you. Drink in the beautiful arena in which you play. Flow with the wind, and listen for the sounds of dogs barking below, or a baby crying in a backyard playpen. But listen to yourself, your madly racing heart, your parachute, the wind, the sky, the planet below. Imagine for a moment yourself to be the first visitor from another star, alighting on the third planet of star sol, perhaps drifting down by some form of air retardation device.

And when it's time to land, land softly, away from people, away from man-made intrusions to the land, or in a meadow. Listen to the grass crunch under you, listen and feel the canopy in its last struggle to stay afloat. And listen to the sounds of the wind at ground level. Listen to your heart. Listen to yourself.

Indulge yourself a minute or two to do *nothing*. Sit, lay down, sprawl out and drink in again the totality of what you have just done, nay, what gravity and air and nylon has just done for you. Fight the fixed-action pattern of behavior which requires you to rush back and pack up *right now*. Enjoy the moment. It is precious. It is timeless.

When you have sated yourself with your emotions, your feelings, with the memory of the golden moments past, when you realize you have taken time to find yourself, and enjoy what you have just done, then again perhaps, if you must get on with *doing something*. But if you do, you might find something is missing. You might find yourself desiring again to MAKE A SKYDIVE.

Appendix

Sources

Now that you have the desire for that training course and your big first jump (which everyone remembers no matter how many numbers they have logged after that), you may not know where to turn to make that first commitment to the sport. The following are parachute centers which are Affiliated Centers which subscribe to training policies and procedures established by the training committees of the United States Parachute Association.

These centers offer the first jump course by certified Instructors; the novice jumper is guided in the aircraft by certified Jumpmasters.

These centers are roughly comparable to ski centers. They also offer new and used gear for sale, rigging services and other services to novice and advanced sky divers.

There are many other sport parachute centers which offer the same basic training course, leading to the first jump, yet are not officially affiliated with the United States Parachute Association. The U.S.P.A. does, however, publish annually an international guide to jump zones, parachute centers, clubs, and facilities. It may be that there is a parachute club or commercial center (which usually offers more aircraft and services) in your area that is listed in the annual. The *USPA Drop Zone Directory* may be ordered by mail from the United

States Parachute Association, Washington, D.C. (Complete address in Bibliography). $2.00

Your local Federal Aviation Administration (F.A.A.) office, located at most major metropolitan airports, will also have the addresses of all local parachute centers, because sport parachuting is, in part, governed by the F.A.A. Owner-operators of smaller airports may also know the location of the nearest sport parachute center, as will many newspapers, and some local library officials.

The best guide to the addresses of all sport parachute clubs and centers, however, remains at the U.S.P.A. national office.

Fayard Aviation, Inc. of Alabama
Box 219
Elberta, AL 36530
205-986-8117

Central Arkansas Parachute
  Center
Box 103
Carlisle, AR 72024
501-982-4692

Antioch Parachuting Center
Antioch Airport, Long Tree Way
Antioch, CA 94509
415-757-9957

Surf and Sky Sports of Monterey
225 Lighthouse Ave.
Monterey, CA 93940
408-372-3088

Perris Valley Paracenter
2091 S. Goetz Rd.
Perris, CA 92370
714-657-3904/657-8727

Borderland Airports Center
4627 Vista St.
San Diego, CA 92116
714-421-9292

Taft School of Sport
  Parachuting
500 Airport Rd.
Taft, CA 93268
805-765-6159

Reynolds Air Service
Littleton Airport
Sedalia, CO 80135
303-794-9390

Deland Air Sports
Deland Municipal Airport
Box 1657
Deland, FL 32720
904-734-5867

Cental Florida Parachute Center
Star Route, Box 498A
Eustis, FL 32726
904-357-7800

Sunrise Sport Parachute Center
RT. 2, Box 217-A
Fernandina Beach, FL 32034

Sun Country Sport Parachute
  Center
5423 11th Ave.
Ft. Myers, FL 33907
813-936-5635

Skydive, Inc.
28700 SW 217th Ave.
Homestead, FL 33030
305-759-3483/247-7526

Swamp Hollow Parachute Center
Rt. 6, Box 13
Quincy, FL 32351
904-875-2767

Ft. Gordon SPC
1924 N. Leg Rd. No. 8-G
Augusta, GA 30909
404-738-0467

Dalton Georgia Sky Sports
Dalton Municipal Airport Rd.
Dalton, GA 30720
404-278-4700

Jump Hawaii
206 Lagoon Dr.
Honolulu, HI 96819
808-261-2879

Ozmo Parachute Center
Rt. 1, Box 63-S
Athol, ID 83801
208-683-2821

Cargo-Air, Inc. SPC
c/o Newark Airport
Rt. 71
Newark, IL 60505

Archway Sport Parachute Center
227 N St.
Sparta, IL 62286
618-443-9020

Greene County Sport Parachute
  Center of Kansas
Rt. 2
Wellsville, KS 66092
913-883-2535

Greene County Sport Parachute
  Center of Kentucky
Rt. 2, Box 140
Bardstown, KY 40004

Greene County Sport Parachute
  Center of Louisiana
Rt. 1, Box 677 E
Dovington, LA 70433
504-892-9998

Descent Sport Aviation
Brantwood Golf Course
Rt. 213
Elkton, MD 21921
302-366-8172

Pelican Sport Parachuting, Inc.
Rt. 1, Box 17
Ridgely, MD 21660
301-760-2422

Southern Cross Parachute Center
Box 366
Williamsport, MD 21795
301-223-7541

Le Jump Pepperell
Sport Center Airport
Rt. 111, Box 601
E. Pepperell, MA 01437
617-433-9948

Taunton Sport Parachute Center
45 Howard St.
S. Easton, MA 02375
617-823-3682

Turners Falls Sport
Parachute Center
Industrial Blvd.
Turners Falls, MA 01301
413-863-2016

Sturgis Sport Parachute Center
Box 127
Sturgis, MI 49091
219-562-3406

Parachuting Service Inc.
197 Burt
Tecumseh, MI 49286
517-423-7879

Mid-Missouri Parachute Center
Fulton Memorial Airport
Fulton, MO 65251
314-642-3186

Expert School of Parachuting
4220 No. 11th
Lincoln, NE 68521
402-477-5577

Parachute Associates, Inc.
145 Ocean Blvd.
Box 811
Lakewood, NJ 08701
201-367-7773

Ripcord Paracenter
c/o Burlington Cty. Airport
Medford, NJ 08055
609-267-9897

Wyoming Cty. Parachute Center
RD 1, Box 174A
Arcade, NY 14009
716-457-9680

Albany Skydiving Center
Duanesburg Airport
Box 131
Duanesburg, NY 12058
518-895-8140

Special Forces Europe Parachute Club
Flint Kaserne Bad Toelz
Germany, APO, NY 09050
08041-30-616

Gift of Wings Skydiving Center
4539 McKinley Pkwy.
Hamburg, NY 14075
716-457-9719

Drop Zone Parachute Club
Fulco Airport, Rt. 67
Johnstown, NY 12095
518-762-4900

Seneca Sport Parachute Club
RD No. 2, Box 2632
Seneca Falls, NY 13148
315-568-2423

Frontier Skydivers
3316 Beebe Rd.
Wilson, NY 14172
716-751-9981

Astroid School of Sport Parachuting
Box 295
Clemmons, NC 27012
919-765-9204

Eastern Carolina Military Parachute Center
Box 2032
MCAS Cherry Point, NC 28533
919-466-2667

Franklin County SPC, Inc.
Highway 56, Box 703
Louisburg, NC 27549
919-496-9223

Franklin County SPC, Inc.
Midland Field
Highway 601
Midland, NC 28107
704-888-5479

Raeford Parachute Center
P.O. Drawer 878
Raeford, NC 28376
919-875-3261/875-5626

Greene County Sport Center of Gallipolis
Box 91
Bidwell, OH 45614
614-245-9339

Waynesville Sport Parachute Ctr.
4925 N. State, Rt. 42
Waynesville, OH 45088
513-897-3851

Skydiving Inc.
Wilmington Air Park
Wilmington, OH 45040
513-398-2955

Greene County Sport Parachute Center of Xenia
1790 Foust Rd.
Xenia, OH 45385
513-372-6116

Skydance Inc.
Tahlequah Municipal Airport
Tahlequah, OK 74464
918-456-5114

United Parachute Club, Inc.
Swamp Pike & Rt. 663
Gilbertsville, PA 19525
215-323-9667

Maytown Sport Parachute Center
722 Basler Ave.
Lemoyne, PA 17043
717-255-2292

Appendix: Sources

Fayard Aviation, Inc. of
  South Carolina
Box 236
Moncks Corner, SC 29461
803-899-2885

Austin Parachute Center
Box 59180
Autin, TX 78751
512-272-5711

Skydivers of Texas, Inc.
5301 Parkland Ave.
Dallas, TX 75235
214-824-3540

American Parachute Center
FM 485
Hearne, TX 77859
713-279-3861

Spaceland Paracenter
Houston Gulf Airport
Box 152
League City, TX 77573
317-337-1713

Para Ventures Unlimited
Slayton Municipal Airport
Lubbock, TX 79423
806-762-8054

American Parachuting
  Enterprises
4209 Cedar Elm, No. 169-B
Wichita Falls, TX 76308
817-691-3251

Ogden Sky Knights
Box 9343
Ogden, UT 84409
801-392-1557

Hartwood Para Center
Hartwood Aviation, Inc.
Rt. 6, Box 369B
Hartwood, VA 22471
703-752-4784

Buckingham Florida
  Parachute, Inc.
Orange County Airport
Orange, VA 22960
703-672-5700

Quantico Skydivers
U.S. Marine Corps Base
Box 344
Quantico, VA 23134
No phone

Issaquah Parachute Center, Inc.
1500 12th St.
Issaquah, WA 98027
206-392-2121

Hassfurt Sport Parachute Center
167A Zollner Strasse
08600 Bamberg
West Germany
0951/32182

Southern Wisc. Skyhawks, Inc.
18300 Winfield Rd.
Bristol, WI 53104
414-857-2007

Sky Knights
Box 817
East Troy, WI 53120
414-642-9933

Para Naut DZ
9096 Highway 21
Omro, WI
414-685-5995

St. Croix Valley Skydiving Center
Box 363
Osceola, WI 54020
715-294-2433

The following magazines and books may be of value to jumpers and prospective jumpers...

Magazines

Parachutist, monthly bible of American jumpers. $20. per year for new membership in United States Parachute Association; $18. renewal membership. Single copy of the magazine: $1.50. Published at: U.S. Parachute Association, 806 15th St., N.W., Suite 444, Washington, D.C. 20005.

Skydiving, tabloid newspaper. Published every three weeks during the year. $12.50 for one year, $20 for two years, $28 for three years. Published at: P.O. Box 189, Deland, Florida 32725.

Spotter, formerly concentrated on jumping in the northeast United States, now contains a broader perspective. Bi-monthly. Published at: 654 Washington St., Braintree, MA 02184.

Books

Barrata, M. Lynn. *Love in Free-fall*. Millbrae, California, Celestial Arts, 1974. Poetry and photography about jumping and being in love.

Beck, D. G. *Guide to Proper Selection and Use of Load-Bearing Parachute Hardware for Sport Parachuting*. Privately printed, 1975. Technical pamphlet about load-bearing strengths of metals used in parachute harnesses.

Caiden, M. *Silken Angels*. New York: J. B. Lippincott, Co., 1964. History of parachuting, from military to sport skydiving.

Colby, C. B. *Chute! Air Drop for Defense and Sport*. New York; Coward-McCann & Geohegan, 1973. Largely pictorial, juvenile account of military and civilian jumping.

Drought, James. *The Gypsy Moths*. Norwalk, Conn.: The Skylight Press, 1964. (Later reprinted as a Fawcett Crest paperback.) Fictional treatment of barnstormers and their lifestyle. Later made into a feature film with Burt Lancaster in the lead.

Dwiggins, D. *Bailout.* New York: Crowell-Collier Press, 1969. History of parachuting.

_____ *Barnstormers.* London: Grosset & Dunlap, 1969. History of early barnstorming.

Emrich, Lynn. *Complete Book of Sky Sports.* New York: Collier Books, 1970. Discusses sport parachuting and skydiving, as well as flying, gliding, and ballooning.

Greenwood, J. R. *Parachuting for Sport.* New York: Sports Car Press, 1962. Beginners guide to sport parachuting. Now somewhat out-of-date.

_____ *The Parachute from Balloons to Skydiving.* New York: E. P. Dutton & Co., 1964. History of parachuting.

Gregory, H. *Parachuting's Unforgettable Jumps.* La Mirada, California, Howard Gregory Associates, 1964. History of sport parachuting, contains good coverage of military and competition jumpers and many stories of one-of-a-kind or unusual jumps. First edition titled *The Falcon's Disciples.*

Gunby, Russ. *Sport Parachuting.* Denver: Jeppensen and Co., 1972. Now in its fourth printing, this book has been, since it was first published in 1960, the most popular beginner's guide to sport parachute jumping.

Horan, Michael. *Index to Parachuting.* New York: Garland Publishing Co., 1977. Exhaustive reference guide to books about parachuting. Index to published magazine articles has hundreds of citations in 59 categories.

_____ *I/E Course.* Santa Barbara, California, Poynter Publications. Guide to passing the Instructor-Examiner course.

Keech, Andy. *Skies Call.* Crawley, England: Beric Press, Ltd. 1974. Exceptional pictorial-poetry work.

_____ *Skies Call II,* 1979.

Kittinger, Joseph (with Martin Caidin), *The Long, Lonely Leap.* New York: E. P. Dutton & Co., 1961. History of Col. Kittinger's test jumping from high altitudes, including the story of Kittinger's 102,000' balloon jump.

Lewis, Gary, *ParaCommander Handbook.* Privately printed, Skokie, Ill., 1976. Guide to the ParaCommander, the most popular parachute ever introduced for sport jumping.

Lucas, J., *The Big Umbrella.* New York: Drake Publishers, 1973. History of parachuting.

Poynter, Daniel. *Parachuting Rigging Course*, Santa Barbara, California, Poynter Publications. Guide to passing the governmental tests for a rigger's rating.

_____ *The Parachute Manual*. Santa Barbara, Poynter Publications. Technical guide to all aspects of parachute design, rigging, repair.

_____ *Parachuting Manual with Log*. Santa Barbara, Poynter Publications. Basic guide to beginning aspects of the sport, with logbook, in pocketsize format.

_____ *Parachuting, The Skydiver's Handbook*. Santa Barbara, California, Poynter Publications, 1976. Basic guide for the beginner or intermediate parachutist.

Rankin, William H., *The Man Who Rode The Thunder*. Englewood Cliffs, N. J., Prentice-Hall, 1960. True story of a fighter pilot who bailed out at high altitude and was pitched around in a thunderstorm, under canopy, for over 30 minutes.

Rossetti, Steve. *Relative Work for Skydivers*. Austin, Texas, privately printed, 1976. Exceptional guide to RW techniques. Worthwhile searching for, if out of print. Many consider Pat Works and Steve Rossetti's book to be the two best books for RW technique.

Ryan, Charles. *Jumpmasters Handbook*. Washington, D.C., The United States Parachute Association, 1972. Basic guide to responsibilities and techniques of the sport jumpmaster.

_____ *Sport Parachuting*. Chicago: Regnery & Co., 1975. Basic guide to modern sport jumping.

Sellick, Bud. *Parachutes and Parachuting*. Englewood Cliffs, Prentice-Hall, Inc., 1971. General guide to sport jumping. First edition titled *Skydiving*.

Shea-Simmons, Charles. *Sport Parachuting*. New York: Pittman Publishing, n.d. Originally published in London, this is a general guide, written by a leader in British sport parachuting.

Valentin, Leo. *Birdman*. London: Hutchison, 1955. Autobiography of early jumper who believed that he could fly with semi-rigid wings. Valentin was later killed jumping wings of his own design.

Whiting, Charles. *Hunters From The Sky*. New York: Stein & Day., 1974. History of the German parachute corps in World War Two.

Works, Pat. *Parachuting: The Art of Freefall Relative Work.* Fullerton, California, RW Underground Publishing Co., 1975. Has introduced many new concepts to RW jumping. Invaluable to advanced sky divers. An impressive book.

Works, Pat and Works, Jan. *United We Fall.* Fullerton, California, RW Underground Publishing Co., 1979. Follow-up to *The Art of Freefall RW*, contains new techniques and philosophies of large-formation RW jumping.

Catalogues

Many firms will send free catalogues; others will charge a nominal fee, sometimes refunded upon purchase. Many jumpers learn about styles in gear by reading the catalogues first. These firms are major leaders in mail-order sales.

Dean Westgard Parachute Enterprises
2627 Nida Way
Laguna Beach, CA 92651

GQ Security Parachutes
P.O. Box 3096
San Leandro, CA 94578

Poynter Publications
P. O. Box 4232
Santa Barbara, CA 93103

Pioneer Parachute Co.
Pioneer Industrial Park
Manchester, CT 06040

Sky Supplies
Rt. 1, Box 894-A
DeLand FL 32720

Relative Workshop
1050 Fliteline
DeLand, FL 32720

Strong Enterprises
11236 Satellite Blvd.
Orlando, FL 32809

Rodriguez Parachute Systems
6107-A Yadkin Rd
Fayetteville, NC 28303

The RW Shop
Route 13
Brookline, NH 03033

National Parachute Supply, Inc.
RD 6, Fairview Dr.
Flemington, NJ 08822

The Chute Shop
Highway 202
Flemington, NJ 08822

Parachute Associates
145 Ocean Ave., P. O. Box 811
Lakewood, NJ 08701

ParaFlight Inc./S.S.E., Inc.
5801 Magnolia Ave
Pennsauken, NJ 08109

Mid-Ohio Parachute Co.
6969 Worthington-Galena Rd.
Worthington, OH 43085

ParaGear Equipment Co.
3839 West Oakton
Skokie, IL 60076

The Jump Shack
45620 12 Mile Rd.
Novi, MI 48050

Joe Smith Parachutes
P. O. Box 39
Lewisberry, PA 17339

McElfish Parachute Service
2615 Love Field
Dallas, TX 75235

(Judy Pszenica photo)

About the Author

Thomas Fensch began skydiving in upstate New York in spring, 1974. Since then he has jumped out of almost everything jumpable from Cessnas to DC-3s. As this book was published he had over 350 jumps. He received his SCR (number 7557) jumping with the Seneca Falls Sport Parachute Club, Seneca Falls, N.Y. (and was rewarded with a beer bath near the hangar after the jump). He has held the USPA jumpmaster rating, but currently prefers RW jumping.

He holds a PhD degree in Communications and "in real life" is on the faculty of the University of Texas. He and his wife Jean live in Austin.

www.ingramcontent.com/pod-product-compliance
Ingram Content Group UK Ltd.
Pitfield, Milton Keynes, MK11 3LW, UK
UKHW022228230426
12048UKWH00016BA/1124